T0196924

PRIMAL WORDS
SELF, LOVE, GOD, JESUS

JOHN CORRY

PRIMAL WORDS
SELF, LOVE, GOD, JESUS

iUniverse books may be ordered through booksellers or by contacting:

iUniverse
1663 Liberty Drive
Bloomington, IN 47403
www.iuniverse.com
1-800-Authors (1-800-288-4677)

ISBN: 978-1-5320-8740-0 (sc)
ISBN: 978-1-5320-8741-7 (e)

Library of Congress Control Number: 2019917649

Print information available on the last page.

iUniverse rev. date: 11/14/2019

DEDICATED

To all the philosophers including: Derrida, Heidegger, and John
the beloved disciple, who wrestled with the Word within the words

APPRECIATION

Betty; wife, editor, and joy of my life, and to those sometimes mystified friends who offered insightful comments and corrections:

Shela Oakley Roberts
David Bates
Elizabeth Johnson
Renee Crauder
Kathy Lidle (now Dolan)

Finally to Father Hubert Beaudoin, Norbertine artist and spiritual director, who kept me in touch with the angels of my better nature.

"Originally the truth of the word is not... 'steady' or 'fixed'... rather it shimmers."

Christopher Smart

"Every word breaks forth from a center and is related to a whole...
Every word causes the whole of language to which it belongs to resonate and the whole view of the world which lies behind it to appear. Thus every word carries with it the unsaid... that brings a totality of meaning into play without being able to express it totally."

Hans-George Gadamer

"In the beginning was the Word... [which is] the real light that gives life to everyone."

Gospel of John

CONTENTS

INTRODUCTION

First a plea for patience. Since I'm working from a twenty year old printed text transcribed first into a non-editable form (PDF) and then into an editable form (doc.X) I can't always control formatting specifics like line spacing and margins. The large open spaces between items, and the annoying line of letters running down the left margin have been largely eliminated. Also I'm using an older malevolent computer who is constantly deleting words, sentences, and sometimes whole passages. My own formatting is quirky enough so if you appreciate the typographical weirdness that's me, and if you don't blame it on the malevolent computer.

A word on who is speaking. Mostly the author, John; some short quotes from notables like Plato, Nietzsche, and Derrida a hopefully now neglected twentieth century French skeptic who separates the author from his or her works (the text) in order to deconstruct – intellectually undermine – their primary line of thought…. *John?* Yes Lord? *Move on….* That was the inner voice of love, Jesus for me, who's sporadic Interruptions keep me focused on what needs to be said. The work looking back is either one of the most spontaneous and creative I've written, or the most disjointed and annoying. I, John, engage in an ongoing conversation with a gay truck driver whose knowledge of the philosophers John is interested in: Plato, Derrida, Heidegger, Nietzsche, etc. mysteriously increases as time goes on. Other fictional voices who are part of the conversation that breaks out while the author is writing an aphorism loaded post-modern upgrade of Nietzsche's *Beyond Good and Evil*, and Pascal's *Pensees,* include Mary Masseuse a wise and kindhearted masseuse who tries to understand John's elusive intent while the truck driver and John are increasingly at odds over their different political and religious views. Originally a willing student, even a straight man who sets up John's lengthy bits of logic the truck driver eventually finds his own voice which challenges John's spiritually focused line of thought.

John's voice appears in print without quotation marks. The truck driver's voice and other fictional voices appear with quotation marks. The voice of love (Jesus for the author) appears in italics as do the poems which are, except where noted, by the author.

John's intent throughout the twists and turns of the convoluted text is to evoke in the reader the ambiance of four primal words: SELF, Love, God, and Jesus. The first chapter Language in Labor sets the stage for my four primal words which hopefully may inspire the reader to find their own primal words which lie half buried in the wealth of words that clutter up our busy lives.

****

Primal Words is not a memoir. Like Plato did with Socrates in The *Republic* and other works I've incorporated a few real people into a philosophical work: my mother Esther White Yoh, her third husband Harold L. Yoh, and Dorothy Day co-founder of the Catholic Worker, all three of whom died many years ago. Living persons and possibly living persons mentioned in a favorable or neutral light are Betty Jean Corry, my beloved wife, Steve and Doreen Corry, our son and daughter-in-law, David Du Plessis, Marcus Borg, Bill Johnson, Rev. Bruce, Dr. Marie Gatza, Rev. Susan Cody, Rev. Hal Tassiq, Sister McCoy, and Dave Barry. Quotations on the back cover from Derrida, Groucho Marx, and Yogi Berra are clearly from the author. Fictional characters with whom I, John, the author, converse from time to time include an unnamed truck driver, Mary Masseuse, and other fictitious unnamed voices. Biblical quotations from the *New Revised Standard Version* are credited as they appear in the text. Other short quotations from notable public figures are also credited as they appear in the text. The poems that appear interspersed throughout the text unless otherwise credited are by the author.

John Corry, the author, is solely responsible for the content of all characters, opinions, and references which appear in *Primal Words*.

CHAPTER 1

LANGUAGE IN LABOR

·······················⟡·······················

2

A potter fashioned a bowl as a gift to his townspeople. On the way to present his gift a storm swirled around him and he fell, shattering the bowl into a million pieces. Many bits were blown away by the swirling wind, but the potter gathered the remaining fragments, and carried them reverently to the town square. There he carefully arranged the remaining shards on the ground to recreate some semblance of the original bowl.

> "I'm not trying to be obscure," he said to his bewildered fellow citizens. "It really is the best I could do."

When he had finished, a heated discussion on the proper arrangement of the shards arose, and several of the bolder citizens stepped forward to rearrange the broken pieces on their own. The first, using only a small portion of the shards created recognizable shapes that delighted much of the crowd. Others, including more fragments, formed complex patterns which received a smaller measure of approval.

As the little drama unfolded the potter grew increasingly agitated. On the verge of making a scene by kicking over the shards he felt a hand on his shoulder and he stepped back from the crowd and turned his attention to other concerns.

5

If all readings of the text are mis-readings, as Derrida maintains what difference does it make whether I misread the text out of ignorance - basing my comments on a chance remark overheard on the subway - or on a sympathetic attempt, after years of doctorial study, to paraphrase my idol's work, without one dissenting thought of my own, or anybody else? Or have I misread Derrida?

5

"Marx had some good ideas but he didn't understand human nature."

"Freud is so negative. Lighten up."

Of course they may be right but without supporting evidence generalizations are borrowed bullshit.

Maritan would not discuss Aristotle with anyone who hadn't studied Aristotle for ten years, but that's going a bit far.

"Who's Maritan?"

Jacques Maritan was a French Catholic philosopher concerned for social justice. A good friend of Dorothy Day.

"Who's Dorothy Day?"

4

Are you saying my life is anecdotal? That I need more data?

5

A text is a translation by a scribe unfamiliar with the original source.

6

A child constructed an elaborate castle with building blocks. A playmate knocked it down and built another. To spare you, the gentle reader, the trouble of dismantling my castle I've left the blocks randomly scattered to be reassembled as the reader wishes.

7

Whitman spent the last decades of his life rearranging the poems that compose the *Leaves of Grass.* Many scholars prefer the earlier edition. Does it matter? Or is the new arrangement a new book?

8

A charm necklace broke and the trinkets were strewn across the floor. Gathered and restrung in a different order everyone admired the new necklace. Was it?

***

Wittgenstein labored for decades to produce *Philosophical Investigations,* which I read, ponder, and am prepared to offer comment on, after only a week or two. Does this prove what Derrida maintains; that readers are more insightful than writers? That interpretation supersedes the text? That I'm smarter than Wittgenstein?

9½

The sound a dog makes in Armenian is "Ergh!" Anglo-American dogs say, "Arf!" or "Bow wow!" Can we assume therefore, that different species are found in different countries?

That Spanish dogs barking "Huf! Huf!" are a different breed from French dogs who bark "Oua! Oua!"?

10
"Some things can't be seen with a microscope."
W.H. Auden.

12
If letters take on meaning only in words, and words in sentences and sentences in paragraphs and chapters, and chapters in books, and books in the author's total body of work, and the author's total body of work, in the literary-historical context of his or her own time, and the literary-historical period in Gadamer's "fusion of the horizons" i.e. - in the reevaluated context of another historical period is there an even broader frame of reference in which primal words find their ultimate meaning?

13
Derrida holds that words are arbitrary signs unrelated to the things they signify. Still, no one is calling their son Adolph.

14
"We all know that there are words that function merely as signals...and then there are other words that bear witness themselves to that which they communicate. These words are, so to speak, proximate to something that is; they are neither replaceable nor exchangeable."
Hans-Georg Gadamer

8
Are some words irreplaceable? Shimmering words? Primal words? Words beyond the reach of culture and language? Jesus

outside the tomb calling Mary by name? Pascal's revelation summarized in a single word found pinned to his clothing after his death. Fire. Kurtz's last words in the *Heart of Darkness.* The words spoken over bread and wine. The words one uses addressing a husband, a wife, a child, a friend? Must the arbitrariness of language sounds and symbols mute the claim that certain words, or certain words in a particular setting, evoke, or perhaps are, primal reality, i.e. life changing, cultural and religious cornerstones around which lesser words may gather?

16

When I was very young
I thought all ambiguities would merge like orchids
on a word
Say this
I sought the immortal word.

Donald Justice

17

Why do some words and even inarticulate cries from the heart retreat from us as they rise to consciousness? Insisting on their own seclusion can certain words and inarticulate cries of despair or joy have a will, a life of their own, apart from a cultural-linguistic context? The word Rama (God) was Gandhi's last word as he lay dying from a bullet to the heart? The name of the beloved uttered during lovemaking? What does one make of the utterances of great suffering or ecstasy? Howlings under torture and the ecstatic cries of lovemaking? Are they explainable in terms of what we know of linguistics, psychology and religion? Or do they like Kurtz's "Horror" and Pascal's "Fire" intrude from a realm beyond our present comprehension?

17A

Once a concept appears in the text Derrida seems to say a counter concept will emerge: black/white, long/short, fear/ hope. The conflict of concepts leads not, as with Hegel, to a temporary resolution of the conflict in a new concept, a synthesis sure to be challenged by its antithesis and so on as evolving Thought (or Spirit - a fateful equation!) wends its way through history in an intentional manner. Rather, for Derrida, concepts endlessly collide, in a random fashion, leading nowhere in the sense understood by purposeful thinkers like Hegel and Habermas. Thinking is playing with concepts, much as one might play a pinball machine without keeping score. The little silver ball of consciousness just keeps bouncing from one idea to the next to the next to the next and so. Derrida of course would reject the little ball of consciousness (a leftover from Descartes). Rather the texts themselves, the written, not the spoken words, seem to argue among themselves. What Derrida values is the play among texts. Among concepts. The exhilaration of seeing Nietzsche expose, revise, refute Plato or Kant; Heidegger revise Plato and Nietzsche, and Derrida deconstruct all of the above along with Freud, Marx, Kierkegaard and as many others as he has time for in a short life. Part of the fascination of the game is that it is all make-believe. No one is destroyed or killed. Plato continues as part of the game. Only now his truth claims are seen to be suspect; open to a variety of dissenting interpretations. It is an exhilarating vision of the way texts talk to one another.

&&&&

Why don't I find the playful Derrida all that much fun to read? Close readings of philosophical texts may be intellectually challenging, even enriching, but it does entail a certain heaviness that works against the sheer sense of play that Derrida privileges. Derrida's thoughts on play read like a serious thesis which deadens the sense of play; much as essays on humor rarely make one laugh. Which opens... *John?* Yes Lord? *Move on...* in any case for Derrida the game... *John?* yes Lord... One side thought on side thoughts? *Make it short...* Can one have a side thought? An aside, bracketed away from the main flow of the discussion? Why it that Derrida's mucking about is in someone else's motivational quagmire induces a somber tone? To me at least. But that's just my interpretation.

67

Don't you just love the little numbers between items? I do. Marks off each item neatly. Putting each one in its proper place, but the sequential part puzzles me. Must the listed items - Pascal's *Penses* (thoughts) for example, all 923 of them be considered in just that order? Would reordering the *Koran's* 114 suras alter Islamic' theology? The course of history? If the items are meant to be considered in no special order, does numbering them not superimpose a predetermined outcome? As if the first number is where we start and the last number not only concludes, but formulates the intended outcome of the intervening numbers?

17B

Why are negative numbers not included? A cover-up? Or fractions – for incomplete thoughts? What was Pascal's 924th thought? 925th? And if one wanted a short read that summed things up, couldn't one just skip to the last item?

***

Derrida's deconstructive play of texts works well at the aesthetic level. Wordsworth rejects the classical tradition of Dryden, Pope and Johnson. T.S.Eliot rejects Wordsworth. Williams Carlos Williams rejects T.S.Eliot. Each rebelling, as Harold Bloom suggests (pushing off himself against Derrida, his mentor, his father? his nemesis?) against an earlier rival. In painting and philosophy as well, this aesthetic interaction is observable. Earlier masters are critiqued and demoted, only to be taken up by a later generation. Deconstruction, as the skeptical element in creativity, has a long history and Derrida has been perceptive in honing this ancient tool into a formidable contemporary weapon.

But I question whether his attempt to avoid Habermas's concern, that deconstruction leaves little room for a rational and ethical dimension, is successful. Texts can refute, belittle, and destroy one another at the literary level and no harm is done. But when text becomes the basis for action to refute, belittle, and destroy other human beings the results can be horrendous. Certainly Machiavelli, Marx, the social Darwinians, and Nietzsche had a role in fermenting conflict; while theologians such as Augustine and Aquinas, Luther and Reinhold Neibhur also justified violent tendencies in the wider society (the suppression of political and religious dissent, nationalistic and religious wars, and harsh treatment of heretics). Even less overtly political writings, like those of Derrida, by stressing the literary conflict between texts effectively avoid separating right from wrong, which is the primary concern of ethically minded philosophers from Plato and Aristotle, though the Enlightenment notables, to postmodern giants including Habermas, Rorty, and Martin Buber. In short there are serious ethical issues which Derrida avoids.

***

Question. To what extent will, or should, my mental fatigue influence the writing of this fourth response to Derrida's thought? As long as I serve the text faithfully i.e. stay on topic and take time to polish the prose my personal life has no bearing on my writing. Hegel's hiccup, as Kierkegaard objected, or any author's illness, divorce, or any other personal irrelevancy is not permitted to leave a blemish on the abstract text. But I am so tired... Take a nap! Talk to a friend! Journal on it! Put it aside!... Does your life go back and forth like mine between purposeful effort and the unintended lapses, when irrelevant affective components to thought often surface? And why are we talking like this between classes.

***

More thoughts on deconstruction. Critique must feed off text in a way that preserves text. Much as adversaries in a drama depend on one another to keep the play going...

"You're repeating yourself John. Just get on with it."

[Aside) Who is this unruly reader? Not the truck driver nor the inner voice of love, not Mary the masseuse my Anima, my inner feminine friend we'll meet further on. Methinks the fellow doth overstep his mark to intrude so abruptly upon a private conversation.]

Perhaps sire you object to Derrida's line of thought that one author feeds upon another. Nietzsche on Plato's Socrates and Kant; Heidegger on Nietzsche and Derrida on all of the above. Like cannibals. Perhaps you find it distasteful that food with its intestinal unpleasantries detracts from the purity of reasoned thought. Leaves a bad taste in the mouth? Bites off more than...

"Stop! Just stop! I will not take part in this charade any longer until the author sorts out the voices in his head, selects one line of reasoning, and proceeds in an orderly way to digest the various... Alright! That's it! I refuse to be drawn into your little game. I have my own life, my own identity. I will not have you put words in my mouth."

So we come to it at last. It's not about Heidegger. It's just the author sitting refreshed after lunch hoping to entertain you, the reader, so that somewhere along the line the revelations that shape my life, my shimmering primal words, may leak out to be shared with someone I respect and even cherish. Why else would I spend my time reading densely reasoned texts? Weighing ever word - well, every thought, or certainly the main tenor of the thing - to be sure that it does not lie. Does not deceive you. I may puzzle and annoy, but I would not willingly deceive you. On that everything depends. Style - "What oft was thought but ne'er so well expressed" - I admire but do not trust. I look for the writers who will tell me the truth as they understand it. Frost I do not like, or very much admire, but he will share his truth with me. Schopenhauer, obsessed with dark side of human nature, can hardly put one clear thought in front of another, or have I read a poor translation? but he will speak his truth to me. He treats me with grudging respect, he grabs me by the sleeve and will not let me go. Look at it! Look at the pain in the world! The injustice, the cruelty! See how even insects devour one another. How battlefields are strewn with corpses, and hospitals echo with groans and screams in the night. Schopenhauer weeps for the world. Through his anger, arguing with and resentful of mindless optimists like Kant he weeps. I have not read the *World as Will and Idea* for ten years and still Schopenhauer cries out to me above the voices of Nietzsche and Hegel, Heidegger and Derrida, "Well what are you going to do about it? How do you, my solitary reader, respond to what I have showed you?" And I am in anguish standing beside that grim old man grieving over the state of our suffering world. If others would not join our grieving they must find another author for from our grieving emerge the words and images that we would speak into the world's need.

***

"Not in Montaigne, but in myself, I find all I see in Montaigne."

Pascal.

***

"I don't understand myself, only segments of myself that misunderstand each other."

John Ashberry

***

Look for the writers who cherish their readers. Not pander to them, coddle them, but respect them enough to speak the unruly truths that lie like slumbering whales just below the surface of our troubled lives. Denise Levertrov speaks to me with her quaint blend of American openness and old world reserve. A passionate academic. A lady who detaches herself from the protest marches and spiritual searching that engage her life, and seeing me on the edge of the crowd, draws me into the conversation. Font size and spacing of poem below is best I could do.

All these images are true... Not one - Giotto's, Van Eyck's, Rembrandt's, Rouault's...not one is a willed fiction, each of them shows exactly the manifold countenance of the Holy One...

In the poem *Variations on a Theme by Rilke* the poet reaches out to her solitary gentle reader. Can we not feel her warmth, her love of God, glowing within her words? How much more direct could she be? Yet she is not effusive, courting her reader's attention. Rather it is the primal word, the love of God that glows through her words. Perhaps I've said too much already. I sense an awkwardness between us and desperately wish to step back. To take leave of Miss Levertrov and the shattering word - God! - Which has emerged between us.

***

If one took every third entry from the 693 in Wittengenstein' *Philosophical Investigations,* the 296 from Beyond *Good and Evil,* and the 923 from Pascal's *Pensees (Thoughts)* might not one create a composite text? If texts are considered as independent entities, divorced from their authors, why should such a text not be as valid as any other? If multi-source texts become common deconstructive commentary might debate the pros and cons of the single source text vis-à-vis the three contributing composite tri-source text from Pascal, Nietzsche, and Wittgenstein. More condensed versions of the tri-source text might include every 27th, every 71st entry. What would these condensed versions have to say to the less condensed versions? What oppositions? What differances might emerge?

***

The last word the dying person speaks is accorded a special significance. Why? Isn't the real text to be found in the will?

***

A scurry of mice let loose on the palace floor may more unsettle the royal court than a pride of lions roaring at the gate.

***

I tried to speak with Schopenhauer but all I got was a recorded message.
I tried to speak with Schopenhauer but all I got was a recorded message.
I tried to speak with Schopenhauer but all I got was a recorded message.

***

Back to the source! Reduce a flower to its component parts and one is left with minute atoms, which crumble to infinitesimal quarks. Reduce a poem to its basic elements and one is left with a jumble of words which decompose to a pile of markings. Forget the source. Look forward for the context in which the fragmented chaos of quarks and random letters find their meaning. Botany and literature. To what component parts may a human life be reduced? Within what wider context may one human life find its meaning?

***

"You, ah, said some writers tell the truth. Which don't? Of the ones you mentioned."

Well Nietzsche for one. And this may be more the fault of his interpreters than of Nietzsche himself. The European commentators, bracketing Heidegger for now, like Foucault, Derrida and Bataille; though Bataille who owes more to Freud than Nietzsche tends to stress...

"You're losing me, pal. Could you just stick to your own view?"

I hate the son-of-a-bitch! He influenced- advocated? - the atrocities committed under Hitler. Exalting the will-to-power over love for one's fellow human beings he encouraged the worst aspects of individualism. He broke the common morality that holds society together, not for a higher morality, but for a gross, a barbarous, morality. When I see people being tortured in...

"Yeah. Ok. I can see you're pretty hot about Nietzsche. Could we get back to why you think he's not telling the truth? Maybe he is and you just don't want to hear it. It's a tough world out there buddy."

With Machiavelli and De Sade, icons of evil who advocate the claims of the powerful individual over the rest of us, you know where you stand. But Nietzsche is shifty. On the one hand he talks about a "new caste" to "rule Europe" and "breeding a race of masters, the future 'masters of the earth' - a new monstrous aristocracy, built on the hardest self-discipline, philosophical men of violence and artist-tyrants given power by the will to endure for over a thousand years." That's in his journal, but similar polemics are scattered throughout his writings. On the other hand, he talks about overcoming the self, rising above the herd in an aesthetic way. The aristocracy of the talented geniuses of the world struggling against the mediocracy around them. It's hard to get a clear picture of what he really means. Want more?

"No. I get the drift. Anybody else? Maybe just one. How about Heidegger? He sounded interesting. Searched for the meaning to life in Being, without the religious mumbo-jumbo. But keep it simple."

I'm more relaxed talking about Heidegger. I agree he's asking the big question, the important question that gets lost in the distractions of...

"You're starting to drift off again."

Sorry. Where was I?

"You're more relaxed with Heidegger but you still think he's not being honest."

Right. You know he supported Hitler? After W.W.II, he backed off and lumped Nazism with American materialism and Russian tyranny as one of the major obstacles to humankind's search for authentic Being, but he never admitted his association with Hitler. People tried to pin him down but he always weaseled out of a straight answer. That's why I think he's devious. He can't admit to a clear and tragic misreading of history. An error of judgement and morality. Therefore there's no room for forgiveness in his philosophy.

Because no one ever makes a real mistake. One grows into authenticity, positions oneself to become an expression of true Being, by avoiding the inauthenticity of the prevailing techno-materialist culture and by distancing oneself from conventional wisdom, from the inauthentic "They". Salvation comes through the right understanding of reality. I think he's a bit of a gnostic. Knowledge over...

"You're starting to lose me again."

Moral choices, repentance and forgiveness are not his strong suit.

"But knowing what life's all about by proper thinking and understanding is?"

Right.

"I still like him. He sounds authentic. Look, thanks for your time. You've been a big help."

Sure. It was good talking with you. Call again.

***

Language is a loosely webbed net unsuited for harvesting the microscopic organisms on which all life depends.

One blink of an eyelid in the autumn woods floods one's mind with more data than can be processed in a lifetime of words. Scarlet, red, orange, crimson, maroon, ruby, tawny, puce, ochre, claret, Titian, flame and a hundred other terms, still leave unrecorded an infinite variety of subtle hues and shades; each distinctive hue blending into objects who's shape and size defies description. Triangular, oblong, cone-like etc. That's it? One's consciousness simply cannot use words to process what one has seen in one blink of eyelid. If asked we'll say the fall colors are breathtaking, or not the same as last year. Language is a poor instrument for recording the bewildering diversity that confronts us at each blink of an eyelid.

Think of the word smooth. Now run your hand across three or four nearby surfaces. Each is smooth, but are they all the same? Think again. Of feelings. He loves his work, he loves his books, he loves his friend, and he loves his wife. Even in the same context - he loves his wife - does the word "love" mean the same thing? At the end of long day? And is every long day the same? During a candlelit dinner, an illness, a misunderstanding, lovemaking, a quarrel? To what extent do circumstances, and other feelings, interests, fears and expectations alter, the meaning of the words we use to express feelings?

Think of cosmic intuitions that well up when we find ourselves suddenly before a sunrise imperceptibly spreading over the early earth, or sitting alone in meditation. Or seated with others in a deeply involving worship service. How limited words are to catch the variety, the ebb and flow, of our response to such elusive realities.

"I thought we were searching for the immortal word. Or words. Is this your final thought?"

No.

***

"Words are cheap but they don't help. They keep us paralyzed."

Thomas Merton,
monk and peacemaker.

Habermas disagrees. He sees words (as I do) as the only way to challenge poverty, social injustice, and war. Descriptive words fail to capture the perceived realities around us, even the shades of feelings conveyed by words like anger, worry, anxiety, prescriptive words used…

"Back up buddy. What the hell is a prescriptive word?"

It's a word like anger or love used not to describe my feelings but to project an intention into the future. Using words prescriptively expresses universal needs and feelings. "I love my wife," carries meaning in a variety of circumstances. For ethical thinkers like Habermas words are instruments that shape common understandings, decisions, and actions in our communal lifeworld, and in the wider political arena. They are the only means available for confronting institutional injustice, for nurturing a more humane and caring society.

***

What's the difference between a philosophical treatise that unfolds purely in terms of the concepts presented, and the same text that uses iconic authority figures to bolster its line of thought? Intellectually there is no difference. The line of thought is credible on its own merits, without the support of outside opinion, but considered in a more inclusive context there is a great deal of difference. The very names: Freud, Marx, Hegel, Nietzsche, Kierkegaard, even if cited with reference to a minor portion of the discussion, introduce an archetypal dimension. Elemental forces central to our modern epoch are embodied in the names of the illustrious ones much as the classical gods of war, reason, love, greed and lust were once the focusing agents for public consideration of society's agonizing dilemmas.

***

Fallible philosophers. Heidegger, to many the outstanding philosopher of the twentieth-century, cannot answer Rorty's simple question, "Is the Nazi uniform still hanging in your attic?" Nietzsche, who offered himself as the prime example of the Superman, is committed to an asylum where he spent the last ten years of his life. Hegel, illuminating the vast historical sweep of the evolving Spirit (Pure Reason?) comes to the astonishing conclusion that the Prussian constitutional monarchy is the culminating apex of all human endeavor! And, as Vonnegut would say, so it goes.

**

"Who's your audience? Who are you writing for John?"
A bored teenager surfing the web for the immortal word.

"No really."

An aging late 20th century intellectual familiar with the works of fading postmodern French philosophers.

"I'm wondering what Ha-ber-mas is it? might say to all this. As the voice of reason. Keep it short I've only got a few minutes till to my next stop."

He would defend the rationality that Derrida, Heidegger and the rest deconstructed. He...what?

"What's deconstruct?"

Reinterpret - downward. Devalue, demote. People you destroy. Ideas you deconstruct. They're allowed to survive in a weakened condition. Habermas would stress the structural tendency of fragmented, oppositional, language to unite in discursive ethics for communitive action.

"What's that mean?"

That language is the primary way human beings communicate. That if people listen to each other and share their differing ideas they will come to common understandings, common agreements.

"You've already shared that idea."

So? Cezanne painted the same mountain in southern France over a hundred times. All slightly different.

"Painting's different. Cezanne's perspective and the subtle shades of color vary, but Jesus John, repeating the same idea over and over. And after I've seen that mountain three times I'm done."

One more and I'm done. Unlike Heidegger who ruminates on what lies on the far edge of human existence, and Nietzsche and Derrida who see ideas playing together in a rather nasty way, Habermas thinks people can talk together and come to agreements that fit their situation and take common action to improve things in the world.

"He's a liberal. Well, good luck. So he would be what used to be called a philosopher? Someone who still believes we can come up with one view of the world that fits all the facts?"

Not quite. The big picture that includes all aspects of reality that Kant, Hegel and debatably Nietzsche's Will to Power painted is pretty much gone. What Habermas said was don't throw the baby out too; that reason still has a role to play in providing a totality within which other disciplines can wrestle with tough questions.

"Go on. This makes sense."

Well I'm not sure I can do justice to the complexities of...

"So what? It's just you and me. Nobody's keeping score."

Well that's it really. Physics, psychology, politics and all the other disciplines that have taken the place of philosophy still need a place to talk among themselves. And other issues on the fringe of modern life, like death, or what caused the Holocaust, need a place to be considered. The notion of totality, not the completed totality earlier philosophers proposed, but a flexible totality which moves as the times move provides such a space.

"Philosophy provides the conference center where the different sciences can come together, share, argue and learn from one another? Could be an annual affair to keep up with the fresh data pouring in."

It's not just fresh data. It's also a place where claims outside science's domain, or that have been rejected by science, can get a hearing. It's open to considering all kinds of claims, testing their inner consistency and their relationship to contending claims. Using reason, not just to solve problems within the various disciplines, but to take a look at the big picture.

"So philosophy is still looking at the big picture, but its doing sketches rather than a finished painting? Is that it?"

Pretty much.

"Two questions then I got to go. 0 God I missed my turn off. Shit!"

Sorry. I got carried away.

"Not your fault. I'll get the next one. Well, I remember one. What claims doesn't science deal with?"

What's right or wrong, beautiful or ugly? God. What happens after death? Why...

"Yeah. OK. Debatable stuff that can't be measured. Final thought. Habermas' flexible totality sounds a bit trendy to me. Could have morality and truth flip flopping every generation or so, depending on changes in the local customs."

He says not. He says there're universal principles built into language, and therefore ethics (people talking about what's right or wrong) is protected from cultural domination. The Holocaust, or slavery or women's rights, are primarily moral rather than cultural or psychological issues. I'd concur. But he needs to open up totality to deal with the mysteries we mentioned. There I'd agree with Heidegger that Being (or some such notion) is needed to keep the space open for a truth not subject to cultural corrosion. An anteroom where we wait on the lost God that Nietzsche, Heidegger, and Jewish Kabbalists like Scholem and Harold Bloom long for. Or - more likely for me the God of Abraham, Sarah and Hagar.

"I can see where this is heading. Some presence, some spooky outside ghost still visits the world? Yeah, well it's not for me. But everybody's got their own opinion. Look, I'll be in touch.

"Right. Thanks for the call."

****

If all the words in the world were piled on top of one another, like a child's tower of blocks, which word would hold up the rest?

***

"With ten as the worst what's the pain now?"

Seven. Not sharp like toothache. What's my pulse?

"It's up to 42. Just relax. Don't talk. You should go to Hawaii. 80° but not humid. Beautiful. Always beautiful. See that? Like a fish gulping air."

I can't see the blood.

"Only when its colored. There! See! The blue's going in and the red flashes are coming out. I'm going to turn on the sound. It's like a washing machine... When I was a kid in school I was fascinated by the heart. The seat of life. I always wanted to be around working with the heart."

In the Old Testament the heart's the center, the core, of a person. Not the lungs, not the head.

"When people think about the heart they think about being nice. Not smart like the brain. You really should visit Hawaii. You'd love it. It's so different. So beautiful."

***

Application. Select no less than three, no more than five, of the most compelling words in your life. Sit with them until... on their own they begin to converse with one another.

***

"We shall never understand one another until we
reduce the language to seven words

Gilbran.

***

Gandi's last word after he was shot was "Rama." What might your last word be? Why wait? Use it now.

***

(-'s) Bit before midnight with long hours ahead. Tubes tangled up all over my chest and arms. Can't sleep. Feeling panicky. Disoriented. Back's sore. Headache from nitroglycerin comes and goes. Long time till daybreak. Can't seem to focus on things to do to face the long night ahead. Reading President Carter, prayer or rest - Habermas and Bataille beyond me. Praying on my back for hours. Writing. That's about it.

(+'s) That Jesus is with me. You came with the priest when I took the host. What a pleasant surprise. Jesus will guide me in what to do. It's your problem Lord. Help me through the night. I'm alone without a roommate; have no real pain and am getting better with the tubes - which I've lived with peacefully since 3:00 last night…

I'm better and feel better since low time in ER when chest hurt and pulse was 38. Thank you for the peaceful cheerful attitude with the nurses. The woman who loved Hawaii and talked about the heart being nice. And the nurse who voted for Clinton because he cared about the little people. Not the big electrical companies who cut off her electricity in winter, because she was 8$ short on her bill! My day nurse, Diane, who was so helpful all day. And Cheri who's been the same tonight. Who will be outside all night to care for my body?

There' a whole team of people working to keep me alive. Nurses, paramedics, cleaning ladies. Dr.Who who carefully explained what was wrong and what they doing about it. As the world fills in around me, I feel reconnected to the human family. Betty so tired from being with me from 2:00 on last night, until she went to lunch with her friends. Being a half hour late, to bring me this notebook and pen, and four or five books. Eating a sandwich rather than the full meal she was counting on. Doreen calling. "This has *not* been a good year!" only two weeks into

January. Steve's kidney stone last Thursday; Betty's wallet stolen at Border's last Friday after the dentist. Me in the hospital Sunday. The Borders staff were so helpful. Not just processing an incident, but being themselves as they helped Betty adjust, who was in shock over the violation of her Pollyanna nature?

"I trusted him. He was in front of my open purse and I didn't want him to think I didn't trust him."

What bothers you the most?

"It wasn't the money, or the cards. It was having my trust violated. He was so polite."

And then the world filled in around us. The staff looking through every trash can in the store carried us past the deep disruption of our common morality. Back to the deeper rhythms of decency that nurture the wider family; so that we face the disruptions, the midnight isolation and fear of losing all control, in a communal context. And strangers around us come to life as our brothers and sisters. Even the ones who abuse our trust. People with whom we can share our fears and problems and who love us back into life. Thank you Lord for my sisters and brothers.

***

"Therefore, it is not the name itself or the metaphor, but the power is it represents that has the greatest significance for Friends."
Maurine Pyle in the Friends Journal

****

My last word? Too early to say. Maybe the one in the hospital. "Which word was that?"
It's there. Unspoken but there.

CHAPTER 2

SELF

Not the knowing self. Not the self-among-selves. Not the body among everybody. But SELF that wills SELF. Ego-SELF. SELF-sufficient-SELF. SELF-made SELF. SELF-against-selves. SELF-over-selves. SUPERSELF. Complete, unique, over all!

***

Childshark
fullgrown lumbers and flashes
in unfriendly seas.

***

In the beginning was the SELF. And the SELF was with God. And the SELF was God and the SELF became flesh and dwells among us.

***

"The will must live on itself, since nothing exists beside it… every individual… makes himself the center of the world, and considers his own existence and well-being before everything else… He is ready for this to sacrifice everything else; he is ready to annihilate the world, in order to maintain his own self."

"The will must live on itself, since nothing exists beside it… Every individual…makes himself the center of the world, and considers his own existence and well-being before everything else… He is ready for this to sacrifice everything else; he is ready to annihilate the world, in order maintain his own self."

Schopenhauer

***

Plato says Socrates accepted death to uphold the law which even if flawed is still the main instrument of preserving justice in society. Or do other factors intrude? Socrates is an old man, his work is complete. Would he welcome a dramatic ending, a martyrdom to preserve his legacy, his fame among his fellow Athenians? Or perhaps more charitably to preserve his cherished ideas of truth and justice? His midwifery methodology?

Perhaps Socrates is fearful of a painful death and anticipates an earlier more peaceful departure. Does he secretly hate his executioners? Does he wish to leave his blood on their hands? Or is he simply a prima donna, hungry for the leading role in any human drama?

Or did unconscious motives, apart from those suggested precipitate Socrates' willingness to face death? A Freudian death wish, associated with his lifelong argumentative style that denied – that killed – the proposed truths of others at last turned inward? Has guilt for denying his culture's most basic values unconsciously erupted deep in his psyche, paving the way for one irrational act to belie a lifetime or service to reason? Has the instinctive inner lion which Freud uncovered and Nietzsche championed taken its revenge on the lamb of reason?

Perhaps the underlying motivation lies in the unresolved relationship with his parents, his sister, a childhood pet? A friend? On whom Socrates takes revenge in this last desperate act. Or is it not Freud but Nietzsche who sheds light on his murky motivation? The lust for power surfacing despite his high-sounding ideals impels Socrates toward the very act of lawlessness and chaos he deplores? Under the guise of justice a murder! A self-inflicted murder has been committed. A body lies puking and writhing on the hard marble floor! Death reigns! Chaos is unleashed! And with it his final triumph – victory over his enemies, whose names have been swept under the tide of history while he, Socrates, is king! Ruler of Western philosophy for a thousand years! Yah!

"Hey pal. Take it easy. This ain't Shakespeare. Socrates ain't Macbeth. Stick to the point. Motives are murky, mixed, and hard to pin down. Ok. Granted. But Jesus all this stomping around on stage, waving your arms. It's giving me a headache."

You missed the point.

"Which is?"

That even a clearly stated intention, sealed by a sacrificial act, can be misinterpreted. And that multi-causation shouldn't cloud the primary intention. After all Socrates had a chance to consider his own mixed motives before he chose to face his death, rather than accept the escape offered him.

"Not sure about that second thought. He may think he's doing the right thing, but still… you know, like Freud said. But the irony fits. You sure you're ok? I don't want you getting lost in the role. Take deep breath. Relax. You had me worried there for a moment."

***

"Committed when the sensitive part has been hardened, that dark and secret crime is the most important of all because it is the act of a soul which having destroyed everything within itself has accumulated immense strength, and this can be identified with the acts of total destruction soon to come."

Marquis de Sade

***

How can you go out now?
"I promised Mel's kids I'd bring over fruit salad."
But tonight's love night. You said you'd be there.
"I'll be back in time."
Sure. Rushed and tired.

***

"The genitals are the real focus of the will."

Schopenhauer

***

When does self-preservation become SELF?

***

"The public be damned."
President of Standard Oil, Cornelius Vanderbilt

***

MySELF which art on earth My name be praised.
MY will be done on earth.
I crave MY daily egofood.
I am not hung up on guilt trips.
I deliverer mySELF from MY enemies.
I'M in charge! Over you! Over all!
YAH!

***

I think therefore I am." Am what? The self-knowing-self? The SELF-willing-SELF?

***

Rarely does the SELF speak in its own voice. Like an archaic first century heresy its arguments must be reconstructed from the writing of its adversaries: Plato, Schopenhauer, Kierkegaard to mention only a few. And all the religious texts. On this point, with notable exceptions, all shades of political and religious opinion agree; to serve one's own SELF over other human beings is the chief abomination of the race. The fall back option of course is to appear to serve others while looking out for number one.

***

"The self-indulgent capitalization pattern is an annoying distraction."
Tough shit.

***

Dream. A pretty good relation with two guys goes downhill when one pisses on the floor and it spatters on me and he doesn't quit when I complain. I rub my leg against the white linen pants of the other guy and he prepares to beat me up.

Further into therapy the burly thugs were joined by the blue lady, a Buddha-like Sunface, and spacious skies, rooms, and landscapes seen from above. There were also terrifying newcomers: swamp lizards, gnawing rats, giant tidal waves. All these burst with the force of revelation into my inner world.

As I was writing spontaneously one figure however, the Benevolent Biographer, stole into my life as unobtrusively as a new pair of dark socks. The androgynous voice seemed to resonate from somewhere far in space. Whatever my difficulties, my failures, might be the quiet voice assured me, "This too will pass. A stepping stone across the river of life. A turning point. A crossroads."

I began to keep extensive journals to assist the unseen biographer. I pondered and processed, evaluated and re-evaluated until there weren't enough hours in the day to contain my developmental musings.

Someday I was assured all this would be invaluable. What now seemed mundane, even tawdry and downright sinful was, in fact, only raw material for the sympathetic biography that was already being written. "A tragic hero of his time." "A seminal harbinger of hope for the wider community."

My Benevolent Biographer would record the injustices I'd suffered at the hands of my adversaries. Those who had imposed on my good nature would receive their just rewards or be forgiven as I chose. The minor and accidental injuries I may have inflicted on others (if in fact there were any) would be seen in a broader context. My beneficent intentions would easily balance any inadvertent misdemeanors. My strengths would be highlighted, my weaknesses explained, my shortcomings seen as necessary signs of growth in the long curve of my life.

There is no hint of harshness here. The uplift I feel in the presence of my compassionate biographer is almost spiritual. I would, however, hesitate to identify my comforting companion with grandmother's God, whom I first encountered in the big Quaker Meeting house in Atlantic City. Somehow the Benevolent Biographer seems too accommodating for that, too much like an indulgent parent, too much like mySELF.

***

Roleplaying Rosa Park's refusal to leave her seat in the white's only front section of the Montgomery bus: the angry bus driver, the sullen white passengers, the colored people with their mixture of fear and pride and the noble white journalist standing up for negro rights.

The evaluation. "It was my first big story. I wanted to make a name for myself." Does it matter what his motives were? Or don't motives matter?

***

Depending on the reader's mindset all texts, from scripture to bird manuals, may be utilized in service to the SELF.

"Bibles I can see. You can't have wars without someone quoting scripture. But bird manuals? What about political thinkers? Marx and Adam Smith. Keynes and Emma Goldman. Rousseau and Camus. Where's the SELF in society? In the social dimension of life?"

It's there. However society arose; whether through a contract among members to restrain each individual's all-against-all, dog eat dog mentality (Hobbes), or Freud's guilty brothers legislating law and order after killing the father-king, or Nietzsche's compact of the weak to restrain the noble strong, or Marx's whoever controls the means of production controls the society, SELF masquerading as self-serving-others subverts the good intentions of the various subgroups in society: family, religious communities, political parties, nations etc. Weak SELVES unite to protect themSELVES; sovereign SELVES utilize existing institutions for their own benefit.

"How can the SELF be weak? Or plural? The almighty SELF joining with others? Cooperating? It's a contradiction of terms."

Hard-liners like Machiavelli and Neitzche would agree. But even they acknowledge the power of the milder classes to thwart the aims of the mighty ones. SELF comes in many forms. One person dominates a family, a political party, a nation: another avoids confronting the bossy parent or the tyrant's rage, to preserve his or her own skin. Who's to say that both, in their given circumstance, are not serving SELF? Neitzche may not approve but banding together is one way to serve one's own SELF. And someday might not the roles be reversed, and the weaker SELF usurp the stronger SELF's power over others?

"The SELF is not about power? I thought power *was* power over others?

Who's boss? Who gives the orders?"

Not necessarily. Power to serve SELF, given one's circumstances and nature, yes. An artist, a leader, a follower, a parent, a child, a boss, an employee, each wills SELF, serves SELF, in their own way. Some seek money, some fame; some a coveted position; some a less formal role of honor within the group. Some a more secluded private satisfaction. It varies. And, of course, each hides their intent from others, so as not to appear a threat to the communal injunction against SELF. But yes, SELF is drawn to power like a moth to fire. The SELF lives on power and dies without it.

"Where does power come from?"

From individuals consistently utilizing their power position in social institutions for their own benefit. Some from positions of authority; others seeking to survive.

Power also comes from…

"From what?"

From a theological source familiar to people of faith as the one who challenges...

"Hey, hey, hey. I thought we'd ruled out the spooky bits."

Sorry. The individual SELF does have power – creativity, enthusiasm, persuasiveness – but it depends on others to acknowledge that power. Despite Nietzsche's objections the tyrant depends on the obedience of his cowed subjects, the artist on her audience for recognition, the financer on the system he manipulates. Every form of SELF aggrandizement depends on the SELF being able to appropriate power from one's fellow human beings. But and this is critical; but the self that wills SELF is also free to reject SELF. Rather than serve SELF the self may serve others, as Socrates did by giving up his bodily self to preserve justice for others. Or as Dorothy Day did serving the poor for decades in the din and confusion of the East Side in New York. Just as the SELF utilizes the social structures around it, so the self-serving-others may utilize those same structures.

"Social structures?"

The chain of command, top down or shared leadership, establishes the various responsibilities and rewards that each member of the organization buys into in joining the various churches, nations, businesses and so on. And no follow up questions. It can get pretty complicated, but that's the basic idea.

"So there's tension between Self-centered individuals and self-serving-others individuals? Each using the social structure for its own purposes. If Gorbachev and Stalin had contended for the premiership of the Soviet Union the office was available to whoever won the job. So power at the structural level is neutral?" Yes and no.

Forget the no John, which would take us into the spooky realm you've ruled out for now.

"What was that? John?"

Yes?

"I hope you appreciate my dual role here. Sitting at the master's feet soaking up wisdom as well as the skeptical straight man eliciting your sage responses."

O I do, I do. But you must have objections you haven't voiced.

"I do. As you went on about the conflict between SELF and self-serving-others

I wondered if we're not a mix of the two. Good and evil working together and isn't that a healthy thing? Instead of trying to eliminate the SELFish part, maybe each one compliments the other. Blake's satanic energy animates our sluggish benevolent nature. The Tyger energizes the Lamb. Evil and good lying down together."

Well yes and no. Yes we need to love ourselves before we love others. Love others as you love your self comes from Jesus who put personal salvation first before we begin to live in the kingdom of God's love. But also no. Blake's non-rational energy isn't evil. Blake's heart bled for the wretched ones - the chimney sweeps and prostitutes - and his use of non-rational, instinctive forces is far different than Nietzsche's. He admires the energy associated with what good Christian mill owners had demonized as evil. He is not a friend of the SELF. His "Divine Countenance" looks in horror on the dark Satanic mills of Albion, and Blake lends his effort to building Jerusalem in England's green and pleasant land. In his mind the SELFish spirit had so wrapped itself in Victorian hypocrisy that he had to look for the Divine Countenance, not among well fed Christians but among the outcasts, starving artists, the mystics and visionaries. Since the prevailing Christian worldview had usurped the spiritual high ground, Blake was impelled to expose the secluded Divine in impious metaphors.

William Blake is a marvelous figure standing beside this-world-is-all grim realists crying out, "Look! Angels are streaming through the window!" Asked if the sun reminded him of a bright coin he beamed, "O no, no, I see an Innumerable company of the Heavenly host crying, 'Holy, Holy, Holy is the Lord God Almighty." How does a "Just the facts mam" rationalist make sense of that? Blake holds his golden arrows and Chariots of fire close to his chest. "No, no, these are not for the faint of heart; the dark brooders over the human condition who weave their densely textured shrouds around the human spirit. These are for the Divine Countenance who burns with compassion for the chimney sweep, the harlot, the poet bursting with joy that has no name. For our wonderful God. *Le Beau Dieu.*

The beautiful…

"I hate to break in but I did want to get back to the SELF. And how it relates to the mixture. 0 Damn! Here's my turn off. Talk to you later."

***

"What happened to the crazy numbering system? If you straighten it out it I could locate the various items."

It became a distraction from the items themselves so I moved to ***. You do have a point but I'm comfortable with a bit of confusion. Numbers create a pattern that seem to be building to a culminating conclusion. I'm in love with fragments built around a few unseen assumptions.

In a dream I had as a kid - or am I making it up now? Really I can't tell. I was running up an escalator going down, then walking down the escalator coming up. I never seemed to get to the floor above or the floor I'd started from. It was most confusing. But fun."

***

This policy (of military power) cannot succeed through speeches, and shooting-matches, and song; it can be carried out only through blood and iron…. Truth comes out of the end of a gun."

Chancellor Bismarck

***

"How many troops does the Pope have?"

Premier Stalin

***

"Do we really need titles?"

Yes.

"Why?"

Titles speak on behalf of millions of citizens: Premier, Chancellor, President, like the archaic Emperor thunders with a fury unmatched by poor poets and philosophers, who speak only for themselves.

***

***

"I flung myself upon him with insults and as he could not retaliate with his hands tied behind his back, I rammed my flailing fists into his face; he fell down and my heel finished off the work; disgusted, I spat into a swollen face. I could not help bursting into loud laughter: I had just insulted a dead man!"

Marquis de Sade

***

In my senior year in boarding school I responded to an older pale skinned red-haired boy who'd been teasing me for months by pounding his head against the concrete indoor fire escape until several others pulled me away. I don't remember ever speaking to him again but I told my sister not to worry. I knew what I was doing.

***

SELF has a shadow. A silent adversary; the angels of our better nature.

***

"Evil comes into the world as far as man posits it, but man posits it only because he yields to the siege of the Adversary."

Paul Ricoeur

"There you go again. Another religious reference. I hope you won't take it the wrong way but I wonder if your emotions might not be affecting your thinking? Or isn't that a problem for you?"

Sometimes things just pop out. I don't know they're coming, but of course I'm responsible. The outburst on Nietzsche I might rephrase. I winced when I said it, but on reflection I wouldn't change the intent of the outburst. Praising God is also spontaneous, but I can monitor that a bit. I agree it doesn't carry weight unless one is already committed to a religious stance. Still I'm not sure I want to be too circumspect, always translating my primal words into common language I might lose something of myself. But in my own mind? No, I don't mind the emotional response. I have strong feelings about...

"Doesn't emotion cloud the clear picture of reality we're looking for?" Plato and Habermas are clear thinkers, but they're passionate in service to their primal understandings. Even Kant, dry and unduly complex, is passionate about separating knowing from willing, epistemology from ethics. Science from faith. Paraphrasing his thought Kant wrote, "I had to slay knowledge to make room for faith." His zeal in defense of traditional morality, and even certain aspects of traditional religion (Judgement, the Afterlife, and God) in the face of the skeptical Enlightenment of Hume, Locke and Voltaire, sustained him throughout his life. But you're right that none of these philosophers are given to partisan outbursts, like Blake is for example. Temperamentally I'm more like Blake, but lacking his prophetic authority I have to defend my line of thought as at least a viable option, worthy of consideration in the market place of competing ideas. I also think emotions have a valid part in that cultural discussion.

My wedding day was one of the most emotional of my life. But the wedding wasn't about my emotions. It was about our commitment to love and cherish each other on all the days when we might not feel the emotions as strongly as we did then. The act of willing into the future was primary, and since it was a significant act it had an emotional component which I see no reason to suppress. Our joy was an integral part of the day; an implied part of our commitment to one another. To marry, or to take any significant action, without emotion   seems s to me bloodless, almost inhuman.

"Perhaps in marriage, but doesn't emotion get in the way during a philosophical discussion?"

It might help. If the whole person isn't involved, emotions as well as ideas, how important can it be? I do crosswords and light editing with my brain. But when I grapple with contending value laden ideas it takes everything I've got to fight my way through the jungle of conflicting thoughts, emotions, and deep seeded presuppositions to Heidegger's clearing in the forest where I sit with the burst of insight that says "Yes. That's it!" and since I'm religious person…

"Hey, hey, hey. You agreed."

Ok but think how the philosophers in Plato's *Dialogues* and the Talmudic rabbis argued, heatedly at times among themselves without, for the most part, ever losing their commitment to truth. Truth expressed not only in their own understanding, but truth as it might emerge after a passionate exchange. But you sound as if you might have another concern to raise.

"I need to digest this first. Call you back."

***

"The papacy is ours to enjoy. Let us begin."
Renaissance pope's coronation statement

`**

"The just man who is thought unjust will be scourged, racked, bound – will have his eyes burned out; and at last, after suffering every kind of evil he will be impaled. Then he will understand that he ought to seem only, and not to be, just... The unjust lives with a view to appearances….He can marry whom he wills…. can trade and deal where he likes, and   always to his own advantage... At every contest, whether in public or private, he gets the better of his antagonists, and gains at their expense, and is rich... He can benefit his friends and harm his enemies... can honor the gods... in a far better style than the just, and therefore he is likely to be dearer than they are to the gods. And thus for Socrates, gods and men are said to unite in making the life of the unjust better than the life of the just." Plato

"You realize Plato sets up this either/or dialogue only to have Socrates demolish Glaucon's immoral line of reasoning, but I'm interested in the middle ground. Most people act from mixed motives; some just, some not so just. Ok? I don't see how you can separate the two. Sometimes yes. Hitler made some terrible choices; Mother Teresa didn't – most of the time, but it's hard to know most of the time which is which."

Well we have the traditional guidelines like the Ten Commandments and the Sermon on Mount, but I agree sometimes traditional morality doesn't resolve the gnarly specifics of an individual's dilemma. Jean Paul Sartre says we have no ethical guidelines (which I'd dispute); that we must create values totally out of ourselves. He uses the example of a patriotic young Frenchman during WW. II who must choose between caring for his dying mother and going to England to be trained to fight the Germans. Without agreeing I can't help noticing Sartre's self-created values owe a good deal more to Enlightenment and traditional principles of concern for others, than to modern ikons like Nietzsche. The ethical idealism, evidenced in his Marxist commitment to the poor, glows through his gloomy assessment of the post war human condition.

Nietzsche was more consistent insisting the individual not loan his freedom to others but keep it for his own benefit. Perhaps Sartre might agree the real freedom is the freedom of intent, rather than the freedom of action which SELF always preserves for its own benefit. Certainly marrying Betty limited my freedom to act as I wished but since I freely chose to share my freedom with another person this seems to me a more authentic freedom.. Freedom of action, which is constricted by factors one can't control, is only an incidental aspect of the primary freedom; the freedom of intent.

"You lost me with that last bit."

But you like Sartre?

"I do, except *Nausea*. Gross. No choice there.

Mush, no real ideas."

That was my favorite, but I was in a murky place too. I didn't want sharp, painful ideas. I wanted mood pieces to cushion the pain, but I think we're beginning to lose the thread of your concern.

"It'll come back."

***

Conversion is the wedding; discipleship is the marriage.

***

SELF is a stink bomb. Everyone can smell it, but no one can pinpoint the source.

***

"I'm still not clear how the mix of SELFish and unselfish motives applies to a person's life. Some people seem more SELFish than others. But why?"

Most of us are driven by a mixture of motives. We work out deals in our own mind. OK I cheat on my income tax, but I wouldn't steal from a store. I cheat on my spouse but no more than once a year. Almost once a year. We have a lumpy package of mixed motives that we feel suits our situation, which we may update from time to time. From convenience more than anything else. The difference is between those who've made peace with their package of SELFish and unselfish tendencies, and those who have not. While most of us have relaxed behind the borders of our everyday personalities, some like Francis of Assisi and Dorothy Day have ventured again and again beyond the comfortable boundaries of their constricted personalities in service to the angels of their better nature. ***

In consequence of this primary mutual hostility of human beings, civilized society is perpetually threatened with disintegration." Freud

***

Love your enemy... if he speaks English.

***

I cheated on a lab report my junior year in college. I also accepted gifts of money, from time to time, from our family hotel, which I knew excluded minorities. I voiced my disapproval of racism at family gatherings but did not protest the business practices of the hotel. Later when I became a Catholic I confessed to cheating and other personal wrong doings, but I did not think to mention my involvement in racism. Why not? Are my societal sins less culpable than my personal sins? What other compromises with the culture have I made to serve mySELF? What is it that clouds our perception of our involvement in societal SELFishness; while we may be quite clear on our individual acts of SELFishness?

- "That leads to my last question. Again. Where do we find the SELF in the wider society?"

We could look for the fruits of our actions as Jesus suggests and judge the Third Reich or Mafia as social phenomenon dominated by SELF while the early Franciscans, and today's emancipatory movements: for civil rights, workers rights women's rights and gay and transgender rights are imbued by selfless motives of justice and concern for others. But that's not a perfect test, because groups like individuals may conceal their real intentions. And most groups don't stand out as sharply as the ones we've mentioned.

Still, we should be as discerning in our choice of the groups we support, as we are of the individual actions we take. Both may lead to consequences we would on reflection abhor.

"Don't think we'd agree on which groups best serve the country. You're beginning to sound like a left-wing preacher."

Peaching's not in favor today, but some sermons still resonate. Those on the hill by the Sea of Galilee, Mount Sinai, Mecca and Medina; the one at Deer Park. But my brain is getting worn. Call again when you have time.

***

"Men must be either cajoled or crushed; for they will revenge themselves for slight wrongs, while for grave ones they cannot.

The injury that you do to a man should be such that you need not fear his revenge."

"As men love of their own free will, but are inspired with fear by the will of the prince, a wise prince should always rely upon himself, and not upon the will of others."

Machiavelli

***

"His every act centered on self; drinking pleasure with bestial avidity from any degree of torture to another... Henry Jekyll stood at times aghast before the acts of Edward Hyde; but the situation was apart from ordinary laws, and insidiously relaxed the grasp of conscience. It was Hyde, after all, and Hyde alone, that was guilty. Jekyll was no worse; he woke again to his good qualities seemingly unimpaired; he would even make haste, where it was possible, to undo the evil done by Hyde. And thus his conscience slumbered."

Robert Louis Stevenson

***

How many of us like doctor Jekyll…
"Forget Jekyll, forget Hyde. SELF isn't evil. I start with SELF. Just me - what I need and want, and am willing to work for. Listen to this.
'The creators were not selfless. It is the whole secret of their power which it was self-sufficient, self-motivated, self-generated. A first cause, a fount of energy, a life force, a Prime Mover. The creator served nothing and no one. He had lived for himself.'

"Ayn Rand. All that bullshit about SELF being a tyrant. Or a damn sadist. That's beside the point. What I want is to do my thing, not hurt anybody, and keep the fuckin' government and do gooders like you, off my back. I help others out where I can, like what's his name, says. But it's my choice! And another thing. What I'm saying is what made this country great! General Motors isn't in business to 'contribute to the wider community.' They're in business to make money. That's what keeps the country going. Enlightened SELFinterest. Best damn country on earth and don't you forget it."

CHAPTER 3

LOVE

The most critical relationship in life is *not,* as saint Augustine and others claimed, between the human soul and God, but between SELF and love. On this all else depends. Everything! The destiny of the individual, the destiny of the human race, the future of the entire creation. No religion, no philosophy, no national or ideological commitment can obscure the decisive importance of this primal contest of wills.

> "If I have all faith, so as to remove mountains, but do not have love I am nothing... Faith, hope and love abide, these three, but the greatest of these is love." [Corinthians 13: 2, 13 NRSV]
>
> Paul of Tarsus

Think what Paul in *1ˢᵗ Corinthians 13* has put in second place. His own faith in the risen Christ! Jesus alive who spoke to him on the road to Damascus; Jesus in whose presence he was blinded for three days in the most riveting experience of his life. The man for whom Paul faced prison, privation and finally death. For years Paul had preached faith in Jesus as the savior and messiah who would return to earth to usher in the universal kingdom of God on earth. This is what he gives up in putting faith second to love. This vital distinction between love and faith was not forced from Paul. Others would equate faith and love, saying without faith in Jesus as the savior the loveless one would surely would be cast into the horrors of eternal damnation. But not Paul in *1ˢᵗ Corinthians 13*. And not Jesus who welcomed those who served the poor *without* faith into God's kingdom calling them the "Beloved of God". This...

"Preachy John. Short bits. Condense, condense, condense."

Somethings can't be seen with a microscope.

"Nice quote. Whose?"

Auden. W .H. Auden, English poet. Somethings take longer to...

"You go ahead with Paul. I'll call back later."

***

Think of Paul (or somebody else) who in *Ephesians* and *Colossians* preached hope in the cosmic Christ. The pre-existent Christ. Our sovereign source, creator of heaven and earth. And hope in the cosmic Christ who will soon return to earth. Both. Faith in what God has already done and hope in what God will do in the future are placed second to common garden variety love. Of course Paul has faith in the risen Jesus, and hope in God's planet-wide kingdom on earth. But not without love.

And how does Paul speak of love? As the loving fellowship of those who believe in the resurrection and hope for the coming kingdom of God? Or as the mystical unity of humankind? What Melville called the First Congregation? Neither. Paul does not limit love to faith communities or expand love to a mystical universalism. Love has its own requirements but the requirements are not theological. They are practical. Love is patient and kind, not boastful or arrogant; love does not insist on its own way. These are attitudes and intentions, incumbent upon all, available to all. Just simple garden variety love understood by the average citizen as well the most sophisticated among us.

Again, Paul values faith and hope in Jesus with all his being, but when push comes to shove common ordinary love, is what is required of us. Without love our faith, our hope, our prophecy, our knowledge, Paul says, are as nothing. As nothing! Everything: yours and my little future, the future of the whole race, the future of the whole creation depends on love.

There have been theologies which take the Paul of *Romans* as their foundation. And more recent theologies that champion the mystical cosmic Christ. The challenge for our time is to create theologies that preserve Paul's privileging of love without marginalizing the two other abiding elements of Christianity.

1

"Are we going to talk about love or aren't we? You started out OK. How we treat others is more important than God, or Jesus or any of that – excuse me foolishness, before you switched away to make an in-house comment to theologians. Christian's theologians. Academics feeding off the fantasy of…."

You're back? I thought you got mad and left.

"It's a free country."

Yes, to put your mind at rest I am going to focus on love. But you have to remember I *am* a Christian; that may flavor what I say. You can remind me when I've strayed too far.

"Don't worry I will."

***

Love is an internal fact. You cannot see love or taste it, yet it is as irreplaceable in our world as the unseen air.

Most will acknowledge that love, like SELF and our other primary words: God and Jesus, is an internal fact of life. Identifying who has love however depends who is making the identification. Before I met Betty the love poems of Shelly and Keats I studied at college made no sense to me. I thought them overblown, confusing and airy. After falling in love - an odd phrase "falling in love" - like a well with no bottom? - the poems seemed restrained. Sensible. Grounded in reality.

Driving back from our honeymoon in the Wisconsin woods I reflected on the sexual disaster I had just inflicted on my young bride. Unable to provide her with a satisfying physical union, even once, I was disheartened as I visualized the pattern repeating itself throughout our new life together. What if I were never to satisfy her? Then the thought came to me. I had not promised to be an exciting and fulfilling lover, only to love, honor, and cherish Betty Jean. That intention was within my control, whether or not my body ever responded appropriately in lovemaking. That will-to-love, over whatever obstacles arose is what has sustained us for the last sixty-two years.

"Is this appropriate?"

"Put in the children here."

***

Facing Mirrors

Betty sitting on the bed's edge
peers into my face
recording in charcoal my aging visage
on a wide white pad,

while I staring back
transform her soft features
midway between Rembrandt's Flora
and his mistress wife
into words
which will recall to me at least
the image of my artist wife.

Artist sketches poet
writing of artist sketching poet;
like Escher's two hands drawing one another
in one continuous motion.

Back and forth and back over the long years
reflecting blurred images gradually sharpen
bringing to focus
unbearable beauty of beloved first face.
We dance barely touching
in one continuous movement of grace.

***

"I've been thinking."

What?

"Well if I write a postcard home saying 'I'm in Thailand" why can't I write a postcard…?"

An email, a text message.

"Ok a text message saying "I'm in love".

"I'm in love" like "I'm in Thailand" or "We're enjoying our stay in love? Another text message home to let people know where you are.

How would you describe this condition of being "in love" then?

"You're the philosopher. You tell me."

No, I mean it. Where is this exotic country for which lovers forgo their homeland?

"Maybe the place we were raised is not our homeland. Maybe this other country – Loveland? - is our real homeland. And the place we call our homeland is really foreign to our nature."

You didn't find this in Ayn Rand. I think I missed something... Hello? You there?

***

Making love. Like making a cake or coo-coo clock? Just mix the right ingredients, put the right parts together, and presto! Love! Putting two naked bodies together like pieces of a puzzle? But, of course, other parts of their personalities must come together as well. Expectations, fears, feelings, memories, attitudes, must also be fitted together to create the exhilarating union called making love. Paradise on earth! A taste of heaven, as popular wisdom has it. Of all human endeavors sex is the most complex, most nuanced, most demanding and most satisfying. No other act - except prayer – draws from each partner as much skill, tenderness, caring restrain, and unbridled passion as the sexual act. It is the secluded ecstasy, the sacred fire that warms even the poorest among us in our winter world.

Occasionally in the sexual encounter love comes to us as a primal word. An utterance spoken into our routine lives that enlivens and astonishes. In that act of animated nakedness when the clothes are cast aside and the partners, alert and rigid with anticipation, begin the slow dance of arousal, the possibility exists that a new word, a new dimension will visit their erotic ballet. As ordinary dreams are distinguished from great dreams, so lovers come to every encounter, every tenderness, with the hope that a primal utterance will be spoken; the renewing word which is the first step into paradise. A paradise, a dimension, it must be said, that does not take the lovers out of, but impinges on, their world, inviting them into love's task to renew the world, to challenge the unjust, care for the injured and comfort the lonely. The ecstatic gift is a culmination, a release and a reconciliation. It is also an invitation to be a campfire not just a flashlight.

"I thought celibacy a was the higher calling. Saints were the ones who sacrificed their sexuality to serve the wider world?"

The tradition of celibacy which nurtured Francis and Clare, Gandhi and Mother Teresa, is not our only model. Today the need is for more sexually active saints. Lovers whose animating inner word impels them to care for their neighbors. Lovers whose erotic energy overflows to heal and enliven the world around them.

***

T.S. Eliot and Wittgenstein both sacrificed their personal lives to focus on work that would benefit their fellow citizens. Eliot forgoing marriage with the American woman he loved and the literary satisfaction of writing in his own voice - his early letters show him to be a SELFcentered philosopher-poet of immense and often petty ambition – Eliot translated his talent, his pride, and his inner anguish into the impersonal abstract yet strangely compelling verse twice removed from his own experience. It was as if Charles Darwin after a fire destroyed the first manuscript the *Origen of Species* had transcribed his mammoth text from memory, not into his own, but into another language. A language which had to be learned first! Looking back Eliot said perhaps he'd given up too much for poetry.

Wittgenstein also suppressed his own concerns - being a Jew during World War II, being a homosexual - to widen our grasp of language to include other voices than his own. He stepped away from the zealous quest for his own truth in his first great work,

Tractus to listen to the muted and varied voices around him in an even greater work *Philosophical Investigations*. Wittgenstein cleared space in the densely textured world of the Logical Positivists, Bertram Russell and G.E. Moore to make room for ethnic, political, and religious viewpoints (language games) which had been denied a hearing among academic agnostics. Both men wrote, not only for themselves, but in service to the primal word of love which enriched those around them. Emily Dickinson, another New England recluse like Thoreau, wrote endlessly to a world that never wrote back. Only six of her over seventeen hundred poems were published during her lifetime, yet her luminous, quirky vision has widened well the world for her fellow citizens ever since. I've had twelve poems published. Does that make me a better poet than Emily Dickinson?

***

"What does Wittgenstein's being gay have to do with his philosophy?"

I just think it's odd a man as articulate as Wittgenstein should fail to mention two of the most relevant elements in his life. Being a Jew and being gay.

"Maybe it was nobody's business."

OK. Maybe I'm too inquisitive. But I can't help thinking that harboring a divergent element in his own nature made him more sympathetic to diversity in philosophy.

"So you think his sexuality made him a better philosopher?"

And a better person.

"Can I share something?"

Sure.

"I've been gay since I was twelve. It's one of the reasons I called in. I, ah, get to meet guys sometimes that way. But I could see things weren't taking that turn so I just stayed in contact. You don't mind?"

A bit surprised. But no, it's not an issue that...

"Let's get off my personal life, OK? And back to the topic. OK?"

But the topic is love. I'd think your love life might be relevant to our concern. I used my marriage as...

"Yeah. Well, let's let it sit for a while. I appreciate your concern."

Sure... You said a while back that we live in a foreign country. That our real home is "in love". Could you say more about that?

"When you mentioned being in love was like being in Thailand, I thought of an old TV series, *Brideshead Revisited,* where a couple having an affair are accused of 'living in sin', as if sin wasn't a onetime thing, but a condition, almost a place where one chose to live on a daily basis. That phrase, 'living in sin' haunted me. 'Being in love' is another word that intrudes into everyday reality. When I was with Sam, my old Army buddy, we felt we were living in a world apart from the war. We lived in two separate worlds. D'ya understand?"

That's deep. So "being in love" is not my having an inner experience, but on Betty and I living together in another world, while ordinary life goes on around us. Marcel's "intersubjectivity"; Buber's...

"Inter what?"

Intersubjectivity. It means truth is not subject-object oriented. Love isn't something in me for her- for Betty. But something we are part of together.

We live alongside each other in a shared reality. Love is our common homeland.

"But not all the time?""

Yes and no. Yes our sense of living together in our homeland is always with us, but sure we also live in the everyday world. Maybe love is the house we live in moving from one room, one stage in life, to another. Every decade things change, we change, but love is always with us.

"Even if?"

The couple changes too much and they part? Yes even...
John. Move on.

Yes Lord... You still there?

"Just for a few minute. My next stop is just coming up, but first I wonder if you haven't overplayed the joys of marriage. 50% divorce rate in the US tells us something. And the other 50% may not be 'living in love' as you put it either."

The best I can do is quote a friend's comment at the renewal of our vows last week. 'Marriage is a perfect union between two imperfect people who haven't given up on each other.'"

"Nice. I'll think about it. O shit here's my turnoff."

***

"You do realize these disjointed bits and longer pieces make it damn near impossible, for the reader to grasp what you're after? We've had the prelude; where's the real stuff?"

If I could organize the escalating points to build a stairway to Paradise I would, but I don't have all the pieces to work with and I can't reconcile myself to a partial pattern that present the real stuff in a tidy package for readers to take home. Those interested will just have to put the pieces together themselves. Saving some, discarding some.

Mary Masseuse. "I like the format! Bits of logic floating in an anecdotal ocean. Klee! Picasso! T. S. Eliot! Conventional and unconventional insights swimming in the sea of uncertainty because that's the..."

John?

0 Lord not you again!

You've done well but it's time to move on.

***

Being in love? Mulling over the critical phrase we've mentioned "in love," but what of Being... in love? Being in Heidegger's sense of the elusive existence that supports all the little beings. Being that comes through love with all the weight and radiance of existence itself?

"I do hope we're not wedded to one way of looking at love. Love like a multifaceted gem shimmers in a bewildering variety of ways. A kaleidoscope of glittering meanings that refuse to be constricted to one intellectual construct that funnels all reflections toward one decisive insight: "Being", "God", "wholeness" or some less imposing precept. One doesn't catch a rainbow in a net; nor love in web of words."

I'm not wedded to "Being-in-love" as the only way to look at love.. As Paul did in *1st Corinthians 13*. Still, until one of the other glittering meanings takes its place being patient and kind is what makes the most sense to me.

"So you'll remain a Christian until you get better information?"

And you'll hold onto Ayn Rand till your gay experience of being in love jars that wobbly cornerstone loose?

"Can I butt in? I don't know what other readers..."

"Listeners?"

"Listeners are getting out of this, but it sounds like a bunch of bewildering bullshit. Is it a narrative? A collection of aphorisms? A sustained argument or what? Seriously friends the thing is falling apart. Krapp's Last Tape Rides Again. Off in all directions."

"Of course you just made things a bit more complicated buddy. We already have enough offstage commentators."

"It's a free country. But don't worry, you won't hear from me again. I've got better things to do with my time. But you might consider staying focused. Think what you're going to say, and how you want to say it. And don't get distracted by irrelevant glittering meanings. Jesus what a mess."

What a jerk. Don't worry, you can edit him out later."

Maybe he's right.

"Hey, don't get down on yourself. We're dealing with tough stuff here. Remember Hopkins? Nobody published his stuff till he was dead thirty years. Takes people a while to catch on. Don't quit now."

Maybe I am just drifting. Just being too lazy to organize things properly.

"Do you really believe that?"

No.

***

"Why must we promise to "honor" and "cherish" our spouse? Isn't love enough? If we love aren't "honor" and "cherish" superfluous?"

No. They spell out aspects of love we might otherwise have ignored. Honor: to treat the beloved with dignity and respect protects the beloved from disrespect, especially from verbal and even physical abuse from anyone including the promising partner. Even when his or her faults frustrate our expectations we've promised to honor our beloved who may not have earned our respect due to some obsessive pattern, some willful addiction. Even should it become appropriate to separate still we have promised to accord our once beloved one honor and respect.

"And cherish?"

Pretty much the same. To honor protects the spouse from abuse; to cherish gets closer to love. It means we value our partner. Part of loving is to protect one's spouse from disrespect, the other is to value our partner above all other loved ones, to light up when they enter the room to care for them when they're sick, to grieve for them when they are gone to whatever worlds await Without those two supports, to honor and to cherish, even passionate love may easily turn ugly.

***

How can one justify turning from a world in need to seek one's own soul? Taking time off for a personal journey, while Paul's "groaning creation" waits for your response? Jesus said we must love others as we love ourselves. If you're not at peace with yourself how can you help others? What appears to be a SELFish search for one's own soul, or for healing inner wounds, may be essential for a lifetime of service to others.

***

When Cardinal Bernadine was asked why he didn't press charges against a young man who had falsely accused him of sexual abuse the cardinal said he'd always preached forgiveness. Given the amount of lying, stealing, deception, greed, lust, and multifaceted SELFishness in the world, its understandable Bernadine would preach forgiveness rather than love. To a just person one may offer love; to an unjust person one can only offer forgiveness.

***

"But I say to you that listen, Love your enemies, do good to those who hate you, bless those who curse you, pray for those who abuse you."
[Luke 6: 27-28 NRSV]

"Whoever comes to me and does not hate father and mother, wife and children, brothers and

sisters, yes, and even life itself, cannot be my
disciple."

[Luke 14: 26, NRSV]

Jesus of Nazareth

"Is Jesus saying we're to love our enemies and hate our family?"
Sometimes. It depends.

***

"I wish the author wouldn't keep wandering on stage to
rearrange the scenery. It's distracting me from the play."

"I like it. It breaks things up a bit. I get bored with just
one script being played out to its inevitable conclusion." Mary
Masseuse a Christian-Celtic pagan masseuse.

"It creates pseudo-intimacy where we're invited behind the
scenes to listen to the author ruminate on his irrelevant life. As
Shakespeare said, 'the play's the thing'".

"'Wherein we'll catch the conscience of the king.' How can
the author engage our conscience unless we are invited into his
life, to see him wrestling with the issues that matter to us?"

"Well, I think it's embarrassing. He should keep that stuff in
his journal."

"We were talking about it being a distraction, not an
embarrassment."

"The two go together. Once my train of thought is broken
there's room for all kinds of things to surface. Fear, embarrassment,
sometimes even hope. And he did share some personal stuff early
on. That hospital scene and talk about being gay."

"That wasn't him. That was his friend."

"That's what I mean. What's that 'other voice', that Dr.
Watson, Sherlock's docile sidekick doing wandering around on
stage?"

"He's not Dr. Watson. The truck driver's a more even match. Since Freud the alter egos, the docile Watsons of the world, have become more feisty. Like Dostoevsky's Underground Man, or Caliban fresh from the subterranean caves of the Lumpkin proletariat.

"Shakespeare's Caliban's over a hundred years earlier than Dr. Watson."

"You know what I mean. Any way I wonder why there aren't more women involved. Male truck driver, male author, male philosopher. Except Ayn Rand, a really unfortunate choice."

"I'm a woman."

"Well that's two of us."

LOVE - PART 2

"Why Part 2? It's the same subject.'
To break things up. I hate long chapters.

***

"Did Jesus really mean for us to hate our parents?"

For the sake of the stranger. The least. The enemy. Those on the fringe. Yes. Jesus enjoyed weddings, honored his parents, provided for his mother (John 19: 26-27), but our intimate circle of family and friends often acts as a cozy cocoon against the crying needs of the wider family. When this happens, Jesus calls us to hate those who blind us to the needs of the outcast, the enemy, and the poor. It's a shocking demand. One Christians must wrestle with over and over.

"Left wing theology. Liberal bullshit - if you'll excuse my French. I'm sick of losers running the country: minorities, young punks, welfare mothers. What about the working majority? Guys like me. You can keep your bleeding heart social workers and their liberal friends in Congress. What this country needs is..."

If you saw someone wandering in traffic what would you do?

"Hey, it's a tough world. You can't save everybody. I've enough trouble looking out for myself."

You didn't answer my question.

"Sure. I'd help. That don't mean I want to spend my life taking care of people without sense enough to stay out of traffic."

What if the woman you pulled out of traffic was on drugs and pregnant?

"I'd call a cop."

And if there wasn't a cop?

"I guess I'd get her to a clinic someplace."

And if the agency was closed?

"OK. I can't let the kid die. Not the kid's fault the mother's a scumbag. I take her home, give her a good meal. A bed to sleep in. That what you want me to say?"

Yes, it really is.

"Even if I might not do it? Even if you just dragged it out of me?"

We'd have to wait and see. See how you feel the next day, the next week, when you see the next person lost in traffic. And the next"

"That's love? Looking for people in traffic?"

Yes. You'll know which ones are meant to be on your list.

***

I was about six when I wandered off on the beach at Atlantic City to play with a little girl sitting with her family. Then I looked up and saw mother. Her face was flushed, with a look I'd never seen. "Take your dirty Jew hands off my kid!" she hissed. And she led me back to our part of the beach in front of the M.B. Later I asked grandfather who owned the Marlborough Blenheim if there were any Jews staying at the hotel. He said there weren't. He said he regretted it, but the other guests would leave if he accepted Jews. He said the Shelburne next door was the Jewish hotel.

After that I began to notice the Jews at my neighborhood grammar school and the few black kids we had, and the Italian kids. They seemed to be arranged in order, with us on top and the black kids on the bottom with Jewish and Italian kids in-between.

Nobody ever said this. It was just something I picked up. And I began to identify with the little girl, the shy, quiet black kids, and the loud, rough Italian kids, rather than my own family who were running the Marlborough Blenheim.

***

Seeds of unresolved injustice lie buried in every human psyche. Kids see a lot of unsettling events like mom's anti-Semetic outburst. "Morgen morgen nur nicht heute spechen alle faule leute (Tomorrow tomorrow not today that's what all the lazy people say) was a family comment on poor people. Because children are basically powerless to confront the discrimination, poverty, and injustice they see around them or on the media they develop ways of ignoring troubling events. These protective strategies passed on through the family and wider culture convey the subtext of our heritage; along with the democratic and religious values of fair play and tolerance. Children learn to ignore discrimination and injustice especially when it involves their own family and social group.

By devaluing certain groups around them and focusing on the personal goals sanctioned by their family and social class cries for justice come to be viewed as an intrusion. Justice is seen as an unfortunate accident, an interruption, deliberately perpetrated by hostile groups around them; groups who are trying to take something from them. By their enemies.

It's this subtext to the religious and cultural values society professes that Jesus spoke against so sharply. He is far more charitable toward sinners than he is toward hypocrites who've been raised in a culture where what one says is belied by what one does. Speaking to adults who do have power he calls us to plunge into the golden river of goodness that runs through every religion, every culture, challenging us to respond to Paul's "groaning creation".

As children our power was limited; as adults we are *not* powerless. We may not be able to rectify the evils around us, but we can chose to respond. That we don't make that choice is our guilt. The human situation that Camus and Sartre point to as...

"You're repeating yourself."

Sorry.

***

My First Visit to the Catholic Worker.

Toward the end of my senior year at Haverford, 1953, Betty and I visited the *Catholic Worker* on the lower east side in New York. I'd met Miss Day, as she was referred by some co-workers, at a seminar in the Haverford college library with other philosophy majors...

John?

Yes Lord?

Stick to the Catholic Worker visit.

I was standing beside Miss Day on the second floor of the Worker looking down through a large studio window at the line of shabbily dressed men below waiting for their noon meal when

I asked Miss Day why those bums weren't looking for work. I meant it as a descriptive word when Miss Day put her hand on my shoulder and said there were reasons I did not yet understand why the men had come to the Worker's soup line. She was a tall impressive woman; I can still see her ruddy Irish face eyes rimmed with burning compassion for the men below. And oddly enough for me as well.

"As a born-again Christian. I just want to say 'hate' is an unfortunate translation. Jesus Christ loved his family and his country.

We were told to put our family in second place only for His sake. Not for the sake of some secular leftwing political agenda. And by the way your friend Dorothy Day is an old line Commie from way back. And another thing.'

"Sir? Sir, can I interrupt for a minute. I don't know what your religious ax is but you're in the wrong forest. We were discussing love. Apart from its possible, but not likely to my mind, religious implications. OK?"

"May I ask one more question?"

"Anything but, 'have you accepted Jesus Christ as your…?' Hello? He cut off. I've got one. We agree the world's a tough place to live. Powerless to change it why not get on with our lives? Do the best we can for the people we can affect, without going broke supporting people who won't work. Or people half way across the world."

***

Can I share something the Dalai Lama wrote?

"If it's not too long."

"Whether you believe in God or not does not matter so much, whether you believe in Buddha or not does not matter so much; as a Buddhist, whether you believe in reincarnation or not does not matter so much... If as a Buddhist you try to implement, to practice compassion, even if you do not place much emphasis on the Buddha, it is all right. For a Christian, if you try to practice this love there is no need for much emphasis on other philosophical matters. I say this in a friendly way... Thus if you consider the essence of religion, there is not much difference."

I wouldn't dismiss faith in Jesus's being raised from the dead as a purely philosophical matter but otherwise ...

"If love's the essence of religion why doesn't the Dalai Lama give up his religious devotions to concentrate on the essentials? He spends hours every day in complex Tibetan meditations. Why not spend all his time caring for others?

Well some people...

"I know. Need a backup. A bunch of spooky beliefs and rituals to get them going. Today that's fading out. As Ayn Rand says people are acting more on their own."

***

Dream. Four trampy old men are prancing and dancing. Three know each other, the fourth one is new.

***

Dream Walks with George. Back home in Pennsylvania Betty and I go to a series of Dream Walks led by George, a Lutheran shaman. Lying comfortably on the floor eyes masked breathing deeply eight to ten Dream Walkers listen to Indian drum and flute music that takes us to our own inner world.

First Dream Walk. Walking on a deserted road at the foot of Acoma butte an ancient Indian village in New Mexico, I see a circle of dancing Indians. One man beckons for me to join the dancing. It is night and the wind spirit moves over the lone level land. Then the dancing stops and I sit down with the others in silence. I sense a strangeness in the circle. One man pierces my heart with his sadness.

(Later George says the man was sitting on the cliff above me weeping for his dead wife). I look for Quetzalcoatl, one of two spirit guides and sense an eagle above the group. (Later Georg says he saw shamans and holy men in the circle... and angelic presences). Then the Indians begin to move in a circle under the eagle. I join them and am pleased and energized...

"Aren't we, ah, wandering a bit here? I'm beginning to lose you again."

But in another direction? Yes, I think it fits. One of the primary images of human connectedness I've ever experienced.

"Could you boil it down a bit? To let the New Age vapors drift off?"

It would lose the flavor. I admit it's on the edge, but it makes no theological demands and it really does relate to love.

"It'll make some listeners out there happy. Go ahead."

"I'm energized to be dancing. I look down and see oil and paint on my legs and ankle wraps with feathers, and moccasins, and other Indian clothing. There's rain at night, and thunder, but the dance goes on. Then it's morning. The mood lightens as the music lightens. The eagle is a sun and we sit in a circle.

The Second Dream Walk. At night the Indians are dancing again with my mom and dad, Tom Eliot, Tom Merton and others. Lots of others. There is no one outside the circle. Tears come and I smile...

The land is alive with birds twittering and animals peacefully grazing. The sun is like, and unlike, the sun of Theodore Rousseau, a French outdoor pre-Impressionist. Then the sun is a child; doing lively back flips in the center of the circle. I'm worn out from keeping open to the outer music, to the inner vision, and to Talimagala who puts her blanket around me as the tape stops, and gradually we return to the waking world. Ten of us, most smiling and wondering how we can share what we've just experienced.

Mary Masseuse, a Christian-Pagan masseuse

"John. She's already been in the conversation."

Sorry.

I just want to say I can really relate to your last experience. I do spiritual massage and I know the Spirit world still speaks to us today but I wonder how this experience fits with your Christian beliefs. And why you'd seek out such an experience in the first place."

The first night Betty and I visited Wendy and Myrna in…

John.

When we first visited Wendy and Myrna in Albuquerque I was badly confused by the presence of spirits I sensed emanating from the Kachina dolls and other Indian articles in the gift shops. Encountering these figures, and the circle of Indians at Acoma during Easter Week, (several months before the Dream Walks back east) when my mind was otherwise drawn to my more accustomed Christian devotions, was unsettling. I called you (Mary) and you said I might meditate on the Last Supper, (it was Holy Thursday) and ask Jesus about my new inner figures. When I did…

"I thought we were going to leave religion out of this?"

If I could finish, I promise I won't wander off course again.

"Make it quick."

When I did Jesus said two of the inner figures I'd met: Quetzacoatl, an Aztec god half eagle half snake, whom some see as a peaceful Christ-like god, and Talimagala an old, and sometimes young, Indian woman who collects our tickets into the afterlife IE the shawls woven of our good and evil deeds, who were to be my spiritual guides. And they were for the next several years and are still part of the strange and comforting inner circle of friends who come to my aid in troubled times.

The next three items, 113, 114 and 115 belong in the next chapter on God. It's hard enough separating items referring to Love, God, and Jesus without my quirky computer formatting the text according to its own mysterious agenda. Some of which I must admit I've left as is.

A few days after **I punched my college roommate John Kit'ridge in the mouth breaking four front teeth** we drove to his home in Washington, D.C. On the second day I told John I wanted to tell his parents the truth, instead of being the noble friend standing by their son after his clumsy fall down the balcony stairs at the opera house in Philly. He begged me not to tell them and I didn't, but the willingness to tell the truth lifted the mounting burden of guilt I'd been carrying since the incident which had grown from mild guilt and regret at disfiguring a friend (John took particular delight in grinning at me through his gleaming metal braces) to nameless dread. A heaviness of spirit that had its source far beyond reluctant regret for having hurt a friend. It was as if my act, and wanting it to remain secret, had opened a chasm in existence. Sensing myself on the wrong side of the chasm cut off from normal life was intolerable, and pressed me toward a willingness to confess my shameful act. It was I have since believed a prelude to falling in love with Betty that summer and my religious conversion in the fall

"Repentance was part of the conversion experience?"

I didn't think of it that way at the time. It had nothing to do with God in my mind. After the dread lifted I soon returned to my normal life.

"And the two sides of the chasm were?"

SELF was clearly on one side. I couldn't bear to see myself as a person who was acting solely for my SELF and lying about it to others. The other side is less clear. Friendship? Truthfulness? I chose friendship over truthfulness by not telling John's parents the truth but I've never regretted the choice. The key point was to escape this horrible image of myself that surfaced after I hit my friend. I just couldn't bear to be that kind of a person. I had to choose to try and act away from mySELF - for somebody else. Whether it was for John, or for his parents was a secondary issue. I had to be free of this horrible SELF.

"Maybe you were just afraid of your own anger? Your own dark side?"

0 yes. But within that anger, which needed to emerge, was an intent that would have destroyed me. And others. Anger I could deal with later but putting someone else first - allowing the common social network of what it meant to be a decent person to take precedent over my own SELF was what seemed critical at the time.

***

"Was this dread, this inner turmoil, solely related to your conversion? Or did you have similar experiences later on?"

Not exactly. Two years ago, Betty and I visited Andy and Beth, and our adorable - well she is! - Granddaughter Sara, in Marblehead. Andy asked if I'd go with him to the Fine Arts museum in Boston two days later while Betty, Beth and Sara went whale watching off the coast. Savoring the intimacy of spending time alone with Andy, doing something we both loved, I was disappointed when, at the last minute Andy suggested we go whale watching instead. Hurt feelings bubbled up just below the surface, but still I agreed at once to his suggestion. What was the point of objecting if he didn't want to spend time with me as much as I did with him? Putting my unresolved feelings aside, I entered into the outing with as much openness as I could muster. And the whales were truly magnificent.

That night lying awake, after prayer had failed to resolve my distress, I began journaling on my inner turmoil. What emerged was that the parent child roles had become reversed. I was using Andy to father to my own needy inner child! What I'd perceived as intimacy, as bonding between father and son, was in reality an unconscious desire to be reconciled with my own father, who'd left me when I was five. Just after my fifth birthday party. This old wound had resurfaced like one of the mammoth whales we'd seen sporting in the Atlantic to almost wreak havoc in our little family circle. Not because I couldn't have shared my feelings with Andy, but because, given the press of circumstances and the tangled nature of my emotions, I needed more space to sort things out. To have shared my feelings, without understanding their source, could only have led to recriminations; dumping my murky expectations on my son, and spoiling our visit.

In journaling the pain of losing my father emerged in an imaginative story of Saint Peter's son, who felt abandoned when his father left to follow the prophet Jesus. Writing of the son's angry frustration and his eventual reconciliation with Jesus released my own turgid feelings which began to flow into more positive channels.

Over the next few weeks I found myself reevaluating my relationship with my other four children. I began to see my desire for one-on-one meals at Denny's and long walks on the beach in a new light. In part my intent had been to maintain an authentic and enriching relationship with my children. In part it represented an unhealthy parental relationship in which I was asking them to give me the love and approval I'd missed from my own dad.

"John? You did say your name was John? I don't mean to butt in but what has all this to do with love and SELF? I really do sympathize with your dilemma, and I'm glad things worked out, but it's all psychological. All that unconscious stuff makes the conscious choice between love and SELF irrelevant. Are you saying love is a matter of letting the slumbering whales of the unconscious surface so we can ride them into a more creative life? Without, or even opposed to, our conscious intentions?"

Not quite. The key element for me in this transforming experience was not the surfacing of the whales. The key element was my choice to act against my SELF which had become entangled in a frozen need. The decisive choice was made *before* I had worked through my feelings. You might not credit this but in my mind this choice was only possible because of prayer. But that's another side of the story. Choosing to act against my own desires even as they were enmeshed in what I took to be, and were in part, legitimate motivations to bond with my son whom I dearly love was a critical element. And is, I believe, a critical element in unraveling any psychological dilemma. It was that choice that persisted throughout the day of whale watching and the midnight journaling that allowed for the whales to surface in a creative and even playful manner. I felt energized and renewed. I'd rejoined my normal life.

Later, on the way to the plane Andy made sure we spent several hours at the Fine Arts museum where I thoroughly enjoyed Rembrandt's *Woman with a Golden Chain* and Gaugin's compelling masterpiece *Who Are We? Where Are We Going?*" I should also mention that Andy bought me a lovely art book for my birthday.

***

After visiting the Bruderhof, a Christian intentional community near New Paltz, New York, on and off over a period of eight years Betty and I were called in for a talk with one of the elders. When I shared my desire to draw closer to the community, perhaps with a third extended open-ended visit Jack said, "Betty has come to the Bruderhof with you, against her own inclination, for eight years. What have you done for her?" As we drove home to Philly my heart sang all the way. Praise God. Praise our...

"Hey!"

I know. Love not God. I forgot.

***

"Ayn Rand says we aren't to give up our creative impulses to serve the wider community. She says work is ingrained in the gifted individual and must be pursued and protected from the encroaching demands of others. When we all serve our own needs first society flourishes with advances in architecture, science, especially government Business, etc."

Does the society flourish? Does our free market economy Rand idolizes provide for the welfare of all our citizens? Visiting Andy and Beth in Chicago I heard the C.E.O. of a large corporation give the commencement address at the University of Chicago, School of Business. He said society had always had one dominate institution. The Church in medieval times, the State during the Renaissance and Enlightenment. Today, he said, the time of the Church and the State had passed. Business was the new center of international life. Market methods and values were dominate in the world, over political or religious interests. Art, Education, Science, and Religion he said were dependent now on Business for their survival.

"We own you," he said speaking perhaps spontaneously, and a bit rashly, of the university to the dean who in previous remarks had stressed the contribution of Business to the community as a whole. Profits not philanthropy were the life-blood of Business.

He was ecstatic at the possibilities of opening up new markets in China for his product. He urged the graduates to join the "crusade" of Capitalism. To not be dissuaded by do-gooders and freeloaders from their primary goal of maximizing profits and capturing a larger portion of market share. He was well received.

Afterwards Andy's friends found the dean's speech confused and irrelevant to the 1990's but were clearly energized by the featured speaker who challenged them to become the alert entrepreneurs who would carry Business into the coming century.

The next afternoon, standing on Andy's and Beth's condominium balcony overlooking downtown Chicago, I gazed to the left toward the North Shore with its high rent apartment complexes and gleaming sky scrapers, while on my right lay the congested public projects, the far spreading slum buildings and vacant lots of the South Side and I wanted to ask the C.E.O. of Campbell soup whether there was any relationship between the flourishing North Side with its lakefront skyscrapers high rise apartment complexes and the endless slums of the South Side. I wanted to ask if Business as the dominate institution in society was in any way responsible for the well-being of the whole society, as the Church and the State had been in an earlier era. I wanted to ask if Capitalism which had been so generous in its support of education and the arts, might not take up the challenge of helping to make the South Side as livable as the North Side.

"Equality? Is that what you'd like? Leveling income so everybody's the same? Take away people's incentive? Well, they tried that in Russia and it didn't work. Sure, it'd be nice if people worked for the common good. But except for war they won't. Most people have enough trouble just working for themselves and their families. No government hand-out program's gonna change that. You inherited your money. I had to work for mine.

You wanta be poor? There's room in my old neighborhood with drug addicts and winos. The guys who sleep till noon, and teenage mothers lined up for food stamps and welfare checks. Sometimes at night in bed I think about the old neighborhood. I see kids I grew up with in a prison cell, or tied to a bed in the ER. The old people peep out from behind cheap curtains, afraid to go out even to shop for food. I don't know what to do. All I can do is keep going. I'm a writer you know. That's the second reason I called in. I was looking for intellectual conversation to stimulate my brain."

What are you writing about?

"It's a novel about gays in the army. It's about Sam and me. About our life in the army and the trial when they kicked us out. Dishonorable discharges. What we shoulda said if the lawyers hadn't gotten in the way. How our love was as good as anybody elses. I'm using flashbacks of gays in the military: Jonathan and David, Laurence of Arabia, Alexander the Great. Faggots who weren't afraid to fight for their country. We were good soldiers, Sam and me. Real good. We were in Nam for three years. I got two medals. We went through a lot together. I miss him. I miss him a lot... We seem to have wandered off topic again."

Love was the topic.

"Whatever. Look I'll be in touch. Take it easy."

***

Pacifism.

In my mid-twenties, sitting on the adobe roof of our Quaker work camp in an impoverished Mexican village, reading Tolstoy and the Sermon on the Mount, I was visited with a riveting sense of unity with the whole human family. The idea of killing a sister or brother was suddenly unthinkable. I'd been raised a Quaker and after years of feeling excluded by the high demands of being a C.O. my whole perspective changed. I saw pacificism, not as a sacred calling reserved for saints, but as a small first step toward caring for the wider family. I was just as angry, just as flawed as before, but at least I thought I won't have to kill anybody. It was a huge relief.

Now I could begin the long process of relearning how to relate to the world around me; knowing I could never be pressed into a situation where I would have to kill anybody. I didn't know where this would lead, but I knew the riveting vision of connectedness to other human beings had altered my life in a decisive way. I sensed the world widen around me as new energy began...

"Goddamn! A pacifist! I might have known. Just... I just want to know how you can excuse yourself from defending your country when she needs you. Nobody likes killing, but Jesus Christ, if we'd just laid down Hitler would have won the war! And you'd be in concentration camp."

During the first few years as a pacifist Gandhi was my model. Non-violence did work in India, in the South under Dr. King. There was real change in South Africa and Poland when people used political pacifism, to achieve freedom from oppression. Since becoming a Christian my views have changed a bit. Now I'm not so sure nonviolence is the answer to every conflict. I respect the sacrifices made to defeat Hitler. I realize I owe my high end standard of living to those sacrifices, but I heard a different calling. I think of Jesus and the martyrs. It didn't work for them. Sometimes evil does destroy good people. That's the risk I run in being a Christian.

That's not my intention. What I'm...

"But that's the result isn't it?"

Yes, that's the guilt I carry. That for the sake of my religious beliefs I would not oppose a Hitler with force of arms.

"I can't decide if you're dangerous or just irrelevant."

I hope I'm dangerous. I hope people like Bishop Tutu, and Dorothy Day, and Dr. King are dangerous. That they do challenge the violence that brings so much suffering into the world. But perhaps *I am* irrelevant. I hope I can live with that too. I'm not trying to be relevant. Just faithful to that first step I took in Mexico forty years ago.

"I don't understand how someone could not come to the aid of one's family and neighbors when we're in a war. Just let them be killed by a Hitler. I just don't think that's right."

Would you want me to go against my conscience?

"I don't know. Really, I just don't know. I'm still a bit shocked. I never met a pacifist before, except the ones who screamed at us when we came back from Nam. We stayed in. Sam and I. Reupped right after the war, but they caught us six months later. Nobody in Nam gave a shit. They needed us to fight their fucking war. But later we weren't good enough for them. It still hurts. But I love the Army. I'd do it all over again."

***

"If you can't love Hitler, you can't love anybody."

A.J. Muste, leading peace activist in the 1960s.

***

SELF in Society.

"If it's clear the basic conflict is between SELF and self-for-others i.e. love, and if most people and most groups reject SELF and support love, why is the world in the mess it's in?"

The commencement speaker at the University Of Chicago School Of Business doesn't speak for everyone in business. Many like the dean see business making a positive contribution to society. And most Americans really do want a better world for everybody. Why then does the SELF-seeking-SELF seem to be winning the conflict with our generous impulses? Why are wars and slums, crime and poverty seemingly insolvable problems? At one level there is tremendous good-will present in the culture. Our democratic institutions do provide us with voting rights, due process, freedom of speech and so on which were designed to encourage a society where love, the common connectedness of citizens, is a significant value, and people are protected against the socially destructive intent of the SELF.

Think of it! 280 million people and somehow food is raised and distributed, children are educated, the sick are cared for, crimes are punished, laws are formulated and for the most part obeyed, public parks are open, libraries are free. It's an incredible achievement. The problem is each institution has its own needs aside from the general welfare. Hospitals must make money as well as cure patients, faith communities…

"And so on. Get to the point."

Every group utilizes the notion of love for its own well-being, *and* its own advancement. The dark side of one's love of country, religious community or other favored institution is that in the cultural conflict between groups one feels empowered to knowingly or unknowingly misread and vilify opposing groups. Psychologists like Freud and Jung speak of projecting the unpleasant tendencies in the individual and in the collective psyche onto an outer enemy. All this is done in the name of love, and its supporting virtues justice, and freedom.

"Why supporting? Can't freedom and justice stand on their own?"

No. It's a longer line of thought but basically freedom means respecting the freedom of our neighbors to life, liberty and the pursuit of happiness. Behind this foundational principal is the assumption we have an affinity for our own species. That we're one human family which ultimately is grounded in love. Narrow freedom is focused on our own…

John?

Justice without love is also unthinkable. Imagine isolated individuals sitting at their computers and electronic devices having their food delivered automatically, their health needs met by robots, and being able to reproduce without contact with another human being. Perfect justice, perfect equality, but no contact no love. We need human contact from infancy to old age. Without love babies die. We all die in one way or another. Love is the sun that brightens the dark universe. Especially the human family.

"But if SELF masquerades as love how can we tell the difference?"

Mary. "John's right that *"Corinthians 13* is our best guide but if we locate patience and kindness…"

And it's supporting virtues: justice and freedom…

"…In our own ethnic, national, and religious communities and demean or demonize our adversaries noble words become weapons in what Hobbes called 'the war of all against all.' But if we look beyond our ingrained ethno-centric, ego-centric world view we'll see the flaws in our own attitudes and behavior and the goodness shyly glimmering from our dreaded adversaries."

"Just for the sake of argument, let's say we don't detach ourselves from our ethno-centric roots. That we don't sit cross-legged meditating our egos away. Let's say we keep our roots, our ego. As a place to begin. Where else we gonna start from? Take Sam and me. I didn't plan to fall in love with a guy. In this society? I'd be crazy. But there it was. Sam wasn't the first guy I had sex with. But he was the first I found myself caring about aside from the sex."

Go on.

"Well I got to Sam via - you like that? French. Via some rather steamy encounters which had nothing to do with love and everything to do with SELF. But the SELFish needs came first - and are still part of our relation. What's left of it? So if SELF is where we all are, maybe we can't avoid it. Maybe we need to accept it - yeah, that's the way I am! - and go from there."

Let life carry you past the SELF into caring for someone else too?

"Works for me."

***

Mary. "Can you hear me?

Yes.

"May I ask the truck driver who called in about Sam a question?"

Sure.

"Sir I was wondering if you encountered John's SELF in Viet Nam.

"Sure lots of guys came out looking out for number one. Kept to themselves, couldn't wait to get home. Three weeks later those same guys would crawl through enemy fire to save a buddy. Every day! Every damn day me or my buddies. That's love. All the rest; the brass, politics back home? Who knows? So many buddies I lost. So damn many died. I... I.... [Weeps].

"Take your time. I'm sorry. I'm really sorry."

Long pause.

"How about you ma'am? How do you deal with your, ah, meaner motives? Your SELF?"

"Well I meditate. I just sit quiet and let thoughts come up. Sounds silly after what you've been through."

"No, go ahead. I can listen too. I had to out in Nam. Take your time. I'm interested. Really."

"Well I sit. Forty minutes a day. I meditate and let whatever's on my mind come up. A nagging toothache. Seeing my daughter for dinner. Being snubbed by a friend. Like geese crossing the sky I let the fears, hopes, and little resentments cross my consciousness. In from the left and out on the right while I focus on the sky and let the geese go by. When the sky's clear I get a fresh start. I become really interested in my clients; thinking of ways to make it a good experience for them. Ways I can relate to my mother that bring us both some peace... I reconnect with my life apart from old expectations and fears. I feel calm, relaxed, and not afraid anymore. Of course the next time I have to start all over. But it helps. Must seem pretty tame after what you've been through."

"No. No. Hey, whatever works? Doesn't sound screwy to me. Good talking to you ma'm."

""What about you John? Do you meditate like the young lady?"

First I want say how moved I was by your conversation with Mary Masseuse. Your conversation reminds me that if we can't change the situation we can...

"You haven't answered my question."

I know. I don't know why... Maybe I'm waiting for Mary.

"I'm here, John. I've got a few minutes before my next client. Please, I'm eager to hear your response."

I don't have one. Not on the topic.

"Which was love unencumbered by a religious perspective. I have thoughts about God. They're just not your thoughts. Before I cut out I just want to say how much I enjoyed talking to you guys. Really. Some of that stuff on Sam and me hasn't been shared with anybody. Felt good to have you guys listen. I appreciate it."

"Me too. I won't have so many geese to sort out when I'm sitting next time... John, how are you feeling? You sound unfinished."

I do have one regret.

"Go ahead."

My mother was a really remarkable woman. I never got a chance to say that. I can't leave her on the beach screaming at Jews. After the divorce she took us, me and my two sisters to Washington during the war. She got a job in the Pentagon as a G-2 file clerk, but after a week was demoted to the gofer pool in the basement. From there mom worked her way up to a G-6 in charge of an office of twenty-five workers in naval intelligence. She could have stayed in Atlantic City with her parents, but she wanted to raise us herself.

Mom was a wonderful mother; raising us three kids, marrying three times, facing family criticism for her divorces. Every spring she swam a mile around Hamid's pier in Atlantic City with Olympic swimmer Ada Taylor Sacket whose name said slowly was my first brush with poetry. Mom loved to sail; taught us tennis, wrote poetry all her life. Esther was her name. Esther Allen White, then Corry, then Gilbert, then Yoh. "Because I kept falling in love Johnny, and every time I did, I had to marry him." Her third husband left her after ten years for a younger woman, after mom had raised four kids from his first marriage, the son of a bitch, and she still kept his picture by her bed till she died. She died at eighty-two four years after suffering three strokes in one weekend. She was swimming the week before but was taking pills from three different doctors without sharing that bit of vital information. Tubes in, tubes out for four months. She taught us to live well even without hope of recovery.

But first I had to break loose from mom. Over politics, over religion, over her picking out my girlfriends. Once she slapped me, hard, just to keep me in line. Once I walked out of our family Sunday lunch in New Rochelle because I was bored with the stupid conversation and wanted to be with my friends back home. I remember Marge saying "How could you? To mother?" I think I identified with my absent dad; it gave me strength in…

John. Move on.

Mom was a great storyteller. We all appreciated her sly humor spelled out on her cardboard ABC board about her close encounter with the undressed old man who roamed the halls at night until one night he climbed into her bed at two in the morning. And of course mom couldn't move. Or talk but somehow she made it sound funny; just another quaint adventure. So many stories she told. The intern at Penn, a college friend asked her to let a few select colleagues see the unusual boil on her back side. When they rolled her into an examination room and drew the sheet back mom turned around to find she was in an amphitheater with three hundred medical students staring at her butt! She loved to listen to the life of the Brownings on tape. She taught me courage and making your life count. My dad was a gentle man. Odd. I learned the manly traits from mom and the feminine traits of caring, listening and gentleness from my dad. I just couldn't leave without telling you about my beloved mom.

"And the fights helped you break out of your SELFcentered cocoon.

Never thought of that. Yeah, I guess they did.

CHAPTER 4

GOD

First encounter? Sitting next to grandmother when I was eight years old in the big Quaker Meeting room in Atlantic City. Grandmother told me we were going to be quiet and listen for God to say something. I thought of King David and the bible stories where sometimes God seemed nice and then sometimes He seemed to lose His temper. Sitting for a whole hour? When I asked who God was she said He might say something through one of the grownups who'd stand up and give a message. God might even, she smiled, speak to me. When I began squirming she changed her approach and said I could think of something pleasant. I thought about being on the beach, sitting half buried in the sand playing with my sand toys and wetting myself as people walked by. And how good that felt smiling and talking with people around me while underneath I had this secret life. Finally the squirming drifted away and I became aware of the stillness around me. All us sitting quietly, grownups and kids, as something I couldn't see settled over us. And I knew God was not in the old people facing me on the front benches or the two big fans overhead, but God was in the stillness. Not just silence but stillness that came out of the silence.

Later the world filled up with other words. Words at college spoken by my revered professors. **Martin Foss** the German refuge, who taught us Kant, Fichte, and Shelling and took care of his wife, who stayed indoors because she was afraid of the Nazis at the door. And Aesthetics. The radiant golden browns of Rembrandt's later paintings were the apex of professor Foss's lectures. From the great soul-filled faces: Aristotle, the mistress-wife, and his own aging visage bathed in dim light emerged the primordial essence that illuminated human beings. When I pointed out that recent cleanings had brightened the dim radiance of Rembrandt's mystic hues I was astonished that Dr. Foss persisted in his defense of the "radiance of life behind all life." And of course he was right.

"I thought we were focusing on God, not autobiographical bits from college." I'm easing my way into the intellectual process that led me to God.

Frank Parker, the second of Haverford's three iconic philosophers was a Neo-Aristotelean realist whose quiet manner and systematic logical thought bemused then irritated our restless late adolescent minds. One Saturday night a group of us gathered around a keg of beer to crack the dreaded Law of Non-Contradiction, the cornerstone of consistency supporting Parker's hobgoblin haven for lesser minds. And we did it! By God we did it! Just before dawn, after hours of intense debate we came upon the spontaneous realization that, Yes! It was an arbitrary hypothesis! An option, Not a binding demand! At last we could get on with exploring the wild meadows of our late adolescent lives. But the next day no one had taken notes; nobody could recall the precise wording of our primal insight, and we drifted back to the drab Aristotelian netherworld where the Law still hung above the entrance. "Abandon hope all ye who enter here."

Douglas Steere, the resident Friend at our small Quaker college, rounded out the big three. A Christian Existentialist Steere challenged us with Augustine's *Confessions* and Kierkegaard's *Purity of Heart* to at least consider the Unseen Presence on whom all life depends. Having bypassed Douglas's Unseen Presence as I made my way through the great philosophers: Plato and Aristotle, Descartes and Hume, Kant, Nietzsche, and Hegel, I found God an archaic hypothesis still locked away under "Existence of..." in some medieval scriptorium.

During the second semester of my senior year while I was being tutored by Frank Parker on John Dewey (my choice) the reigning American pragmatist - "Why would you want to study such an unsubstantial philosopher?" - I attended a guest lecture on Christianity by a recent Haverford graduate attending Princeton Theological Seminary. He was eager to share his conversion experience and recounted philosophically irrelevant stories of how his life had changed. How he'd lost most of his friends but found a new life.

Critiquing his muddled thinking walking back to my room in the dark I thought it's all nonsense of course, but what if there were an intelligence other than human intelligence in the universe? Something or someone, that knew all about me? And cared for me? It was a riveting supposition that overnight took root in my mind and heart. God did exist! Something or someone did know and care about my existence! I didn't have to do it all alone. I had a companion. A cosmic, yet inner, friend, to whom I could take my daily needs and I began to speak to this Unseen Presence and answers came back! I *was* known and cared for. It or He, or whatever God was, would tell me what to do. Day by day and it worked.

***

Note. Poems are especially challenging to font and format. I didn't dare try footnotes.

Praise God Within What Is

I MADE THE EARTH, AND CREATED HUMANKIND UPON IT;
IT WAS MY HANDS THAT STRETCHED OUT THE HEAVENS.

[Is. 45:12, NRSV]

Claims for a sovereign source,
laid aside by Newton's heirs under myth expired
still evoke nostalgic hope
regret that we could not preserve at monkey trial
and Galileo's confrontation with the Church
Assisi's canticle;

God's grandeur leavening the universe.
Sister water, Brother fire
earth and moon, wind and sun
our cosmic genealogy...

***

"God is dead... Religion is the opium of the people... Science has disproved the existence of the supernatural... God is an illusion, a fairy tale invented to comfort us in a harsh world... "Poor Tom is dead to us all...No sensible person in the 20th century can seriously entertain faith in a supreme being" Virginia Woolfe reacting to news of T .S .Eliot's conversion ... a ghost in the machine... archaeology is the proper study for archaic religious practices and symbols. Belief in God is an obstruction to progress and the invincible human will..."

"They"

"Perhaps 'They' are right."

During the high heydays of European Christendom only a few maverick thinkers questioned the wisdom of the common faith. Today those who question the prevailing wisdom of our cultural deities: Business, Science, and Politics often do so in the name of God.

"Doesn't prove anything. Last gasp of a dying faith. Today it's knowledge not faith that seals the deal."

***

...WHO HAS MEASURED THE WATERS
IN THE HOLLOW OF HIS HAND AND
MARKED OFF THE HEAVENS WITH A
SPAN?

Is. 40:12a NRSV

Just before Einstein and Plank
the figures were almost in place
Things are not so certain now.

Caprice of quantum leaps like feisty lambs
unsettles flock;
implies a more elusive realm
fathers-forth what we may weigh.

Space-time bends infinity compacted to a fiery
end and then?
Looking back the other way
one ponders what lay behind the Bang
who lit the fuse with which all things began - again?

Perhaps the myth has not expired.
Uncertainty's a quirky queen.
Is there a chance we yet may sing Assisi's canticle?

***

"My question
Not answered but given its part
In a vast unfolding design."

Denise Levertov

***

John Hick wonders why world religions can't agree on God as the unifying concept, and let the divisive historical particulars fade into the past. No one, says Hick, of good sense would disagree that people of different faiths need to meet and share, allowing the Great Spirit that animates us all to communicate its plans to renew the earth: to heal the sick, comfort the poor, and bring justice to an unjust world. No one of good will, of whatever faith, cann*ot* value Gandhi, Elie Weisel, and the Dalai Lama for their efforts to plough up the hard soil of political reality to plant new seeds. Why quibble over the controversial specifics of each faith? The suffering world lies before us!. There's work to be done.

But many of us need a backup. Unable to extricate ourselves from our dilemmas, inadequacies, and sins, in order to be the loving people Jesus and Buddha want us to be we seek God's comfort and guidance. Well then, Hick might say, take time for private prayer, for common worship in the faith community of choice, but do not cleave to antiquated particulars of your heritage that would divide you from others.

Which particulars must go? For Jews the Law binding G-D to G-D's chosen. For Muslims the *Koran* as Allah's decisive word of Truth. For Christians the Resurrection and divinity of Jesus. For Buddha...

John?

But what's a Jew without the Law? A Muslim without the *Koran?* Just another ancient scripture? Or Christianity without the Resurrection? Just another liberal – or conservative? - Political action group? Does the Great Spirit really want us to discard these troubling particulars in our enlightened age? If the Muslim…

John? Move on

***

…O that we might gaze as Einstein
               Chardin

> *And Pannenberg*
> *at earth and heaven wrapped around us*
> *sustained by God's consistency*
> *bristling with creativity:*
> *Mutations,*
> *quantum leaps*
> *unruly lambs.*
>
> *What new songs might we sing what praise*
> *thanksgiving pour out to expanding splendor*
> *vast beyond the psalmist's dome*
> *So much more to see and praise*
> *than was ever dreamt before.*

***

The word God in human hands. A tool for building one's own house in the crowded global village? A weapon to ward off trespassers? A hammer to smash their fragile homes? In Ireland. In Israel. In…

***

"O my Lord, if I worship Thee from fear of Hell, burn me in hell, and if I worship Thee in hope of Paradise, exclude me thence, but if I worship Thee for Thine own sake, then withhold not from me Thine Eternal Beauty."

Rabia al-Adawiyya

***

"The mix of short and lately longer bits is not coming together for me. It feels like a lot of scenery is being moved around on stage. When does the play begin?"

Talking about God *is* moving scenery around. Setting the stage for the real drama going on off stage.

***

<u>Hearing voices</u>. Hearing an inner voice cuts both ways. It may of course, distract us or even worse urge action dangerously bizarre. On the other hand, attending to the inner auditory leading has been critical to the lives of many: Dr. King, Sufi saints Rabia and Rumi, Rabbi Israel Baal Shem Tov, and millions of ordinary believers.

GUIDELINES:

>>> Most authentic messages are positive. Most are life-affirming.

"Positive is life affirming. Why must you keep repeating yourself?"

I'm a Gemini. I tend to think in dualities. A single word or phrase may not convey the emotional component intended; may only advance the thought. Hebrew scripture is full of parallel phrases that reinforce and deepen shades of meaning taking the reader into an imaginative clearing where elusive insights in uncluttered clarity emerge. The danger is that even a primal word like love or God may be obscured by a flood of reflections.

You may be right. It may be an irrelevant stylistic quirk but it gets my juices going. I do try to weed out the most annoying.

"Once in a while no one minds."

"Can we return to the Guidelines now?"

In a minute.

...Praise God for particle, wave, quark and field foundation on which salvation rests.

For gravity and laws of motion atomic ladders bonding in carbon-rich prehistoric seas. For the long adolescence of sweet mother earth whirling in dark webbed and wondrous skies wanton for the fiery rays of her solar paramour; bursting with green...

Unusual or Radical demands need to be looked at carefully. A friend put off listening to the inner Voice of love for years because she was sure she'd be sent to work with lepers in Africa. When she finally relented she was led to marry, raise a family of four, and provide leadership for a large charismatic prayer community with a ministry to Vietnam refugees and the homeless in Philadelphia. To expect radical or extreme leadings as one's just desserts for a lifetime of vacillating frailty and sin, feeds into the cultural-conscience, Freud's Super-ego, a rigid disciplinarian who is all too eager to usurp the authority of a loving God.

A few radical demands, over the course of a long life, will probably be genuine. Most will not. When we were living, working, and identifying with the poor in the inner city in Philly the Voice whispered, "I didn't call you to be Francis of Assisi. I called you to be John." And later, "... a poet and writer for my sake." But these personal directions never shut out the cries of the poor calling for my attention. Thomas Merton heard a similar word in the turbulent 1960s when racial conflict and war in Southeast Asia was tearing the country apart while Merton continued his cloistered vocation – vacation? – In the Kentucky woods.

I'm not suggesting we ignore our natural outrage at the horrendous events of our time: wars, torture, child abuse and clerical cover up, and so much more; only that outrage not be the deciding factor in our decision-making process. Our task is not to feed the poor, protest racial, gender, and sexual injustice but to listen to the teaching of our faith communities and society's prophetic angels of our better nature, before we listen to the inner Voice of love who entrusts us with our particular portion of the world's suffering.

"Hey. Whoa. What's this 'society's angels'"?

The last book in the *Christian Testament, Revelations,* speaks of seven angels who hovered over seven cities in Asia Minor. Every city, every nation has an angel of its better nature. Ours is embodied in the *Bill of Rights*. With "liberty and justice for all from sea to shining sea".

***

"If you want to do the right thing, no matter what, 'way will open'."

Quaker mantra

***

Paul often lamented his harsh life: long years traveling on dusty roads, his message scorned, beaten, and imprisoned, but Paul obviously loved his calling to build Christ-centered communities of faith. One has only to look at the faces of the Dali Lama or Mother Teresa on television to see the joy and eagerness they carry into their appointed tasks. Now Job, Jeremiah, and John of the

Cross are another story. Most of us, thank God have been spared that particular calling.

***

Sin

"Sin John? Most of us have outgrown that controlling code word for an Evangelical agenda."

Liberals like Dr. King, and Pope Francis use the word too, but if wrongdoing suits you better…

"It *is* odd we call people liars, hypocrites, mean spirited, rapists, murderers, bloodthirsty tyrants, but nobody's a sinner."

***

The false SELF which slips so easily back in place was exposed for me in a dream in which Bing Crosby the archetypal nice guy was exposed as a puppeteer acting behind the scenes manipulating a papier-mache figure I recognized as my SELF.

Early on after conversion the generous heart overflows with enthusiasm to serve the world. Later we may find ourselves striving to look good rather than being good. It's a real dilemma. We are called to let our good works shine before others. On the other hand good works done to make us look good expose us as hypocrites which Christ implies is worse than sin. It's tricky discerning between the call to genuine humility and using humility as an excuse for not doing the clear teachings of the parables and the Sermon on the Mount. That's when prayer and trusted spiritual companions are essential to discern which tendency is right for the dilemma we face.

Even when unconscious motivations have been factored into the discerning process the believer confronts the mystery of a God who is wholly within and wholly beyond common morality.

Once discernment points us in the right direction justice and mercy like a giant tidal wave sweeps into history. First into our little lives and then in the great emancipatory movements of our time in India, Alabama, Poland and the Philippines.

"You're beginning to wander, mixing politics in with ethics and faith. Not my ethics, but at least keep to the subject."

Mary M. "I think that is the subject. It reminds me of Teilhard de Chardin."

"Who?"

"The Vatican silenced priest and paleontologist whose vision of all creation evolving from microscopic sea organisms through eons of change to the first human beings in central Africa revised Catholic teaching on evolution at Vatican II. Chardin's vision of all life, especially human life, leading to cosmic consciousness of God and God's kingdom on earth energized liberal Catholics and cosmic-minded believers like myself to embrace the wider mission to renew the earth through participation in contemporary movements for justice and peace. John, would you agree?"

Almost. I love Chardin's vision of all creation evolving toward a loving relationship with God, but I do have reservations about his sometimes pollyannic reading of history. Accepting nuclear weapons for example, and some of the social disorders he perceives as part of God's unfolding plan leading to the peaceable cosmic kingdom Jesus promised ignores obvious evils that have had a major role in history. Despite flaws Chardin's vision is an inspiring response to traditional sin-saturated Catholic theology, His science based mystical theology was the breath of fresh air Pope John XXIII had prayed for his church at Vatican II. But...

"But what?"

But he seems to ignore the individual's free response faced with divine evolution. And God's adversary who's done a good job so far challenging Chardin's...

"Could we take a break? My brain is about full."

How do we take a break in writing? Insert blank pages?

"Don't you have any short bits you can put in to lighten things up?"

"Could I make a suggestion?"

Sure.

"I could give you both a little relaxation exercise to..."

"Excuse me ma'am but I'm still driving an eighteen-wheeler."

That won't be a problem. Ok? Take a deep breath... And let it out.... In and out, in and ahhh out. In and out."

"Feel better?"

"Yes I think I do."

"Good, now where were we?"

"May I butt in? Please, could you get back to the topic? I'm taking notes on the Guidelines and I'm having trouble with all this small talk in class. The first is that inner messages are generally positive. The second that radical demands are rare. The third is... I forget what the third is".

No surprise there. The third which I edited out is that prophetic words generally affirm the major teachings of the faith community. I did have more to say on the apparent conflict between Chardin, Hegel and Kierkegaard but that's just my opinion."

"Don't bail out now, buddy. Your opinion is your opinion. Stick to it. We don't have to agree but we do need to have something to think against. If you won't stand behind your own insights we're back in Derrida's house of mirrors. I think we can do better."

How?

"By holding to your position and letting the dialogue unfold as the rabbis and Athenians did, searching for truth, which they came upon, or stumbled over, in the course of their conversation."

OK. I withdraw the objection that my Guidelines are purely personal, and problematic on that account. I do mean what I say. But my other objection is that I really do have questions that I don't want to resolve just to fit the narrative and logical needs of a text. Kierkegaard vs. Chardin and Hegel, for example, on the role of the individual in history.

"Can we get back to the Guidelines? I may be just a note-taker but I am looking for help in my scattered life."

Sure. I didn't mean to... "Just get on with it!" "Don't listen to him." "I do appreciate your attention to my concern..."

***

Contemplation

Some of us are called away from the active life to serve God in silence, until silence gives way to stillness where the world is left behind and we are at one with God; two spirits in one space. Responding to God's calling with an open heart, being energized by the Divine Presence becomes the primary reason for living and we, as Christians, begin the long interior friendship with the risen and pre-existent Christ. Think of it. Seven billion human beings on earth and God...

John.

Yes Lord.

Move on.

And then God sends the contemplative a sea of troubles to hold in prayer. And that becomes one's task! To hold Paul's "groaning creation" against one's troubled heart. With God. No one could even for a moment carry such a burden alone.

Mary M. "But sometimes God leaves the room and I'm left alone with the burden, and I have to believe against all the inner evidence that God is still present. Contemplatives like Mother Julian of Norwich and Teresa of Avila, your favorite Saint John, and Thomas Merton carried such a burden. Merton, like many literary saints from the Gospel writers to Augustine, Teresa and John of the Cross, was given the gift of speech as a writer as well as the gift of silence as a monk, wrestled with this dual calling most of his life. It all depends."

"I'm really lost with most of this stuff. Could you help me out here?"

I'm afraid I'd just repeat myself. I would like...

"I find it helpful. A bit limiting but each person must find their own path up the mountain. What I miss is the broader vision that includes the Great Spirit's wondrous manifestations among Asian and Primal peoples. And the sense of cosmic energy, compassion, pulsating throughout creation. The older view of divinity as person - I have problems with Yahweh - seems limiting."

The difference between those who relate to the Divine as cosmic compassion, and those who relate to the Divine in Buber's I-Thou terms is not as sharp as it sometimes seems. The Divine is associated with both energy and relationship. Still the distinction is useful. I find myself led to address the Divine in a personal way. As God, as Father, as Mother, as Creator, as friend. I have a harder time relating to cosmic compassion as the Dalai Lama does. I cherish the opportunity to converse with God, alone or with others in gathered worship where we wait upon the primal word to enliven our lives. Each Saturday at Mass or Sunday at Quaker Meeting I ask God for a word to carry me through the week. The temporary word within the eternal word. It's usually a one or two syllable word like "peace", or "sheer joy" or more ominously "patience" or "courage".

"I'm uneasy. The items seem to be getting longer and longer."

If this were a more conventional text would you feel less uneasy?

"But it isn't a conventional text. Once I got used to your format I've come to expect a certain pattern."

Stick with the sense of uneasiness. Of being disoriented. You may never get out now. We may never return to the item format. Does it matter?

•

"Help!"

• ***

Praise God for photosynthesis
Enfolding breath of leaf and lung
Into life with every breath we take.
Praise God for muscle bone and heart;
Nerves running everywhere and brain,
Gullet, gut, intestines,
Secluded genitals;
Body's ballet of moving part
We celebrate with every motion made...

***

Servant and Friend. I often think of God as a boarder who has taken up residence in a remote upstairs room in my house for whom I run little errands from time to time. Sometimes my secluded boarder invites me in for a visit over wine and something to eat. Sometimes we talk, sometimes we just sit together in silence. The rest of the time I go about my normal life, but when the boarder calls I listen.

***

If "Language is the House of Being," as Heidegger claims, where does that leave silence and the One who comes to us in silence? Circling the House like two lost dogs?

***

Discipleship and Adoration. Discipleship takes one up the inner mountain toward the peak. Along the way we come upon a clearing and look up in to catch a glimpse of the radiant peak above. Our hearts open in wonder at *Le Beau Dieu* - our beautiful God - who gleams upon the peak. Many on the slopes farther up than you or I never see the summit. The journey is in the climbing, but joy is at the peak.

***

Encouraging Words. Over and over in the midst of the world's and our own harsh words God's quiet words of encouragement hang in the air. *"Why be afraid, I am with you. I love everybody but you are my favorite." Come after and be home to your creator and true friend. I've been waiting a long time. Rejoice and be...*

"I, ah, thought we were saving Jesus for the next chapter."

Did I mention Jesus?

"You didn't have to."

"He's right John. You snuck one in."

Difficult to avoid. Perhaps you've noticed three of our primal words: love God, and Jesus do overlap.

"Not for me they don't."

Mary V. "Not for me, either."

***

The Holocaust, the Guilty God, and Murderous Evil.

"Hey hey. I thought we were focused on one topic at a time. Short or long. That's three."

It'll be a bit longer than usual, but the topics do seem to be related. Mary what do you think?

"I can see there's a connection. What does our truck driver friend think?"

"Not sure. But since I've put up with God's glory for the last ten pages I'm curious how John deals with the dark side of life. OK if Mary and I break in if we need to?"

I'd rather you limit your comments till I've responded to one line of thought. But yes. You'll break in just as you've always done. How would you start?

"After the Holocaust many Jews, like Elie Wiesel, who wished to retain their relationship with G-D insisted we must now worship a guilty G-D. A G-D who stood aside while G-D's chosen were gasping for breath in crowded sealed off gas rooms. Have you an answer for this revised image of God?"

In a bit, but I have something to say first on primal words. There are no answers to primal words, only life altering responses. The Murderous Evil behind the Holocaust and other historical horrors speaks a word within language that eludes language. To place primal words alongside other words falsifies the reality of these… what can we call them? Intrusions? Riveting encounters? That shatter our everyday understanding. Primal words, life-affirming or life-threating, demand not an answer but a response of the whole person.

Whether it's a response to SELF and Murderous Evil or Love and God we are asked to say yes or no, or sometimes wait and see.

"But not too long. Eventually one either rejects the SELFish option or doesn't, takes action against Murderous Evil or doesn't. Right?"

Right. Mary?

"I agree so far."

"What do your philosophers have to say?"

Not much. Classical philosophers and modern thinkers like Descartes, Kant, and Wittgenstein pursue other concerns, but not Hannah Arndt's Radical Evil. Schopenhauer shows deep appreciation for the terrifying aura of the word. Will as chaos. Nietzsche, even more perceptive in tracing its presence in human existence, is intoxicated by its power, and serves at times as its spokesperson. A stance that many emulate but few would openly advocate.

Artists, writers, and film makers have been far more insightful in wrestling with Murderous Evil. The late Goya, Bosch and his medieval depictions of hell, and more recently, Picasso's *Guernica* graphically depict murderous evil. Greek literature with the *Iliad,* and the terrifying dramas of violence and retribution contrast sharply with the reasoned dialogues and expositions of Plato and Aristotle. Dante and Dostoevsky on the other hand…

Too much, move on.

Theologians…

Keep moving.

Perhaps the reason artists, writers, and filmmakers bring us closer to Murderous Evil is that killing is always personal, rather than abstract which the comfort zone of philosophers and theologians is. It's the images of evil not the reasoned arguments that jar the emotions loose from conventional patterns of thought. Dostoevsky's Ivan agonizing over one murdered child, Raskolnikov killing an old woman to assert his own existence over God, student nihilists of the *Possessed* who prefigure the coming horrors of Stalin's tyranny, Elie Wiesel's eyewitness account of the death camps, Picasso's screaming women in Guernica. These are the images that bring home the reality of the murderous instinct in human life.

"John?"

Yes Mary?

"You haven't mentioned scripture."

I know. The place where evil doesn't have the stage all to itself; the place where there is real conflict between good and evil, God and God's adversary.

"Can you keep it short? I'm almost to my last stop, in Albuquerque. And you might say something about the guilty God."

The first passage that comes to immediate mind is Cain's killing his brother Abel where God protected the murderer from counter violence from Abel's relatives by putting a mark on Cain's forehead; which set the precedent for outlawing capital punishment and protecting human life in a variety of ways.

"And the second?"

The evolution of Satan, God's courtly adversary in *Job*, to the increasing ominous figure who in the Christian tradition is the fallen angel of light, the spiritual personification of Murderous Evil.

"And the guilty God?"

No. I could not worship a guilty God. Recognizing the human capacity for sin and the malevolent figure of Satan I do not hold God responsible for the horrors of history. Human beings misled by the one who was a liar and a murderer from the beginning put the Jews and other enemies of Hitler's Third Reich into the death camps. To have saved the Jews God would have had to renounce freedom and the uncoerced love that flows from freedom.

"Which opens a longer discussion but not now."

Right. In short, a guilty God is unworthy of my allegiance let alone my adoration.

"Thanks. Talk to you later."

***

Mary? What's on your mind?

"Murderous Evil. Not a helpful concept for me."

I shouldn't wonder, the way Satan's been misused to demonize one's enemies: political and religious.

"What's Satan to you, John? How can you embrace such an archaic and divisive figure?"

The one who urges me to acts of violence is a very real figure. Since my mid-twenties I've listened to his hateful rants, and drawn his face in Jung's Active Imagination exercises where the client is encouraged to allow the inner figures to express themselves in spontaneous scribbling, which morphs into variety of inner images Jung called Archetypes figures found in every culture, either secluded in the conscious culture or more openly in dreams and the Unconscious.

I first met God's adversary in therapy. As I reflected on my past I realized that though I regretted certain acts of youthful violence, I also identified with the angry John who relished banging a sneering classmate's head on the stone steps of our dormitory. I was a senior in prep school and for several years was able to control my anger but four years later I woke up hung over after a college beer party to realize I had punched my roommate, John Kit'ridge, in the mouth breaking four front teeth. The dread of carrying unleashed anger with me for the rest of my life led to my embracing God as my defender against my own anger.

The struggle continues to this day in my inner life. When I see soldiers in Sarajevo firing into civilian crowds, or hear of campesinos being beaten in small Latin American police stations

I am not only the victim being beaten. I'm the one in the rumpled uniform standing over the victim wielding the club. Satan's place in scripture only confirms what I experience in my own life and in the murderous violence of my lifetime. Wars, torture...

John?

Yes Lord?

Let the dark figure speak.

DIE. DIE YOU BASTARD DIE. I RULE. I AM KING. AT MY HAND ALL WILL DIE. I RULE. I AM KING OF ALL LIFE ON EARTH! DIE YOU SHITHEAD DIE!

In sharing the evil one's rants, I do not invite a psychological interpretation. I've counseled on my Shadow side in Jungian therapy and out over many decades to separate good Shadow (my repressed resentments and other negative emotions which liberates energy needed for Jung's Wholeness which incorporates all four aspects...

John?

Yes Lord. 90% good Shadow, 10% Satan.

GOD - PART 2

I'm looking for a bridge between the last item and the ones that follow, but there is no bridge between "murderous evil" and Love, God, Buddha, and Jesus. Each side holds its own deep mystery, its own logic; each insists on its own voice, unmuted by the demands of reason for compromise and reconciliation. The insidious hiss of violence would draw us into its own dark whirlpool, apart from the life enhancing primal words.

***

0 God protect us from murderous evil that would silence your primal words of love, joy and service to the sisters and brothers you have entrusted to our care. Renew those of us who have wrestled with the darkness of our own worst fears. Place us in your loving presence which has overcome all confusion, all darkness, and all evil. For you Lord are the mighty one. Our creator and our advocate. And our final home.

***

*...Praise, gratitude, for wide world where
each feather fitted feature of creation
lifts us to your arms O Lord.
Evolving truth unveils elusive overlapping laws...*

***

"On the whole reason remains hostile to scripture."
George Hans-Gadamer

Well yes and no, depending on whether the miraculous is placed within or outside the ring of reason. If it's a completely cause-effect, measurable, universe, then of course miracles have got to go. The notion of an Unseen Presence operating independently of agreed upon probabilities does unsettle the hardy fisher folk trolling with a loose net who miss the microscopic life that feeds the visible food chain emerging farther up. But if reason includes totality, the wide horizon that recedes as we advance, one may entertain the possibility that oddities may yet connect in some meaningful way

If reason is committed exclusively to the measurable dimensions of reality then of course the house is only one story high and we must dismiss rumors of other levels out of hand. But since Freud opened up the basement perhaps an upper level is not unthinkable; an attic, also out of sight, to balance the secluded basement from whence emerge the meaner motives oozing upward to infect those who inhabit reason's well-intentioned, if not tidy, ground floor living room. Perhaps the unseen attic may account for saints; those radiant visitors who seem to have dropped in from another sphere.

Perhaps you find three levels a cumbersome concept? Try this. In the one level living room we stumble in the darkness, colliding with furniture and one another, coping as best we can, until almost by accident, we bump against a switch and regain our innate ease of motion as we move about the room. Adjusting to the well-lit furniture we turn and look at one another as if for the first time; smiling and chatting together. No longer fearful. Perhaps God is the switch, hidden in the darkness, waiting to lend us light.

"Perhaps not. That spooky option expired centuries ago. Darwin, Marx, Freud, and a whole host of scientists who deal in the one real world have long since laid that particular ghost to rest."

Challenging your ikons with my own Einstein had a broader vision than Newton's heirs; saw God's handiwork reflected in the stars. Jung, Eliade and Joseph Campbell illuminated the sacred inner space where humans have worshipped the Divine Nature from Stonehenge to St. John the Divine in uptown Manahattan. Wittgenstein moved past monolithic Marxism pluralizing philosophic uniformity to validate the language games that enhance faith among the varied faithful. Jung, taking a second look in Freud's basement, found the Creator abandoned in a corner and moved God up to the attic open to the stars above. So many others: Martin Buber, rabbi Hershel, the Dalai Lama, Dr. King and Dorothy Day all move us past the intermediate answers into another dimension.

***

Praise God for lichen, moss, and conifers;
for arm wide dragon flies
pterodactyls, turtles, dinosaurs
that still roam the child-like mind.
God's plenty brimming over time.

Praise God you …

"I must say I find it a cheap shot interjecting irrelevant patches of praise in the middle of a serious discussion before we've reached consensus on the validity of their intended subject."

If I waited on your permission I might never sing at all.

"Well you could at least wait until you're with your religious buddies and not inflict it on the rest of us."

Remember that novel you're writing about gays in the military?

"What of it?"

My patches of praise are like your love story to Sam: hymns to my beloved partner. I don't sing to make you uncomfortable. I sing because I'm in love. God is my beloved. Not some stupid concept, some transcendental hypothesis.

"Coulda fooled me. You've spent a lot of time trying to wedge the possibility that belief in God is a credible intellectual option even today."

Pause.

Maybe you're right. Maybe I do share at two levels. Say the theological level and the devotional level. Martin Buber tells how after months of dialogue defending the possibility of God's existence his dissenting partner finally changed his mind. But instead of being relieved Buber is saddened that he wasn't able to share God as Thou, the living God, the primal word.

I feel the same way. I do think intellectually the concept of a caring creator is a viable option and with others I tend to stress that aspect of my faith, but inside it's not just an intellectual assent. It's a love affair. My relationship to God is my rock, my shield, my comfort in distress. God is the Creator who brought me into life from my mother's womb, who comes across the water to hold me when I fall. God is my Sam. My beloved. And I want my beloved's name to be at least respected by others. That I care about. I don't care if you believe or not. But don't demean the name of my beloved!

"Steady on. Who's demeaning your beloved?"

It's done. Look at the media: films, T.V., novels. Listen for references to God. Negative, slighting, offhand. Churches and synagogues are not for weddings or funerals but for services being interrupted; a place where spies or cops or suspects bring their own agenda into God's sacred space. Where religion and God are a way stop on the way to somewhere else. Look at the way clergy are portrayed. Meanspirited high-volume Evangelicals or fuzzy minded utopian liberals. In sophisticated circles one doesn't mention God, or if one does it's always what I think of God, my take on God.

"But lots of clergy *are* meanspirited and air-headed, and isn't that what you're doing? Your experiences? Your interpretations?"

I hope not. I hope my experiences, my thoughts, help clear a space where the primal word God... Lord... Great Spirit... may arise. Where readers sense behind my words the One-who-can-be-trusted. Where the living Word, breaks into their life and they can put down the book unfinished because they have rejoined their intended life.

'You're a mystic."

I'm not an anything. I'm one who loves God and is having a hard time putting it into words. And before you say why bother, why not leave it in silence I must say I have to try. Just like you have to write the story of your love for Sam and the Army, whether anyone reads it or not.

"Fair enough."

What did you say?

"Ok. I guess I can accept that's who you are. I'll try to be less abrasive. I don't like it when people trash gays so I can give you that courtesy."

Thank you very much... So I can use the patches of praise?

"Sure. I'm not the only listener. Maybe someone else will appreciate them."

Joyful joyful we adore you.
Hearts unfold like flowers before you
Opening to the sun above.

Melt the clouds of sins and sadness
Drive the dark of sin away
Lift us to the joy divine
Thou are giving and forgiving
Ever blessing, ever blessed.

Schiller's *Hymn of Joy* that appears in Beethoven's 9th symphony

***

Loving Evangelism. David du Plessis, a marvelous Pentecostal preacher from South Africa, who was instrumental in bringing the Holy Spirit that his tradition cherished to the mainline Protestant churches and later to Pope John XXIII just before Vatican II, cautioned against an overzealous evangelism by saying we were never to witness to a person we did not love. Whether the message is received or not is not our concern. We've been called to share our great joy in God's love. The rest is not up to us.

"But if your truth is the Truth why not present it as forcefully as possible?"

While meeting Jesus face to face is the most compelling experience of my life what I present to others is for them an option, a hypothesis that must be tested by the fears and hopes they carry in their hearts. I'm not so presumptuous as to think I'm the first person to have spoken to them of God. What do I know of the buried treasures they may carry from their earlier experience of the Divine Nature?

Evangelism is dialogue that involves listening as well as sharing our understanding of scripture and our experience of God's love. Any canned or preplanned jargon that would elicit an unconsidered immediate response; anything that smacks of the lawyer or salesperson is foreign to the Spirit that would share itself as love – or not at all.

***

My beliefs as compelling as they may be for me, are in part dependent on history ending according to biblical prophecy. This is why I believe Paul speaks of faith, not knowledge. Should history end in a manner inconsistent with the hope of the early church for Jesus, the Messiah (Christ), to return to usher in the peaceable kingdom of God on earth would not alter my experience of Christ? I experienced what I experienced. But it would change my understanding of other stables of Christian belief: Incarnation, the preexistence of Christ as co-creator with God, and even the Trinity. Christ means messiah and if he isn't the messiah of the end of history it changes things. Not sure how but it does. I act in faith, not in certain knowledge. I see dimly as Paul says; then I shall see clearly, face to face. That's why even to me, my beliefs apart from my encounter with Christ, are in some sense a hypothesis, but a hypothesis to which I cleave if I am to remain a Christian.

***

"Which is it John? Which is the critical event, Resurrection or the Second Coming of Christ?"

It's both. The Resurrection encourages me to have faith in the other major scriptural events: the Incarnation, the Trinity, etc. while the Messiah's (Christ Jesus') future return to usher in

God's peaceable kingdom on earth calls us to have faith that the end of history, like the beginning, is in God's hands. We have faith in Jesus as risen several millennium ago; we have hope for the future kingdom of God, and we have love for God and our neighbor right now no matter what happens.

"You could be wrong."

Not about hearing Jesus say "Follow me."

***

Jews, Muslims, Buddhists and Christians have similar expectations of a culminating historical event (or for Buddhists a culminating event at the close of our particular historical cycle). Just as our belief as Christians in God's peaceable kingdom on earth energizes our present discipleship so others' vision of the glorious end to history draws them like a magnet through their present trials and tribulations. Like scientists with conflicting strongly held hypotheses believers from various traditions must wait on the future for verification of their deepest hopes and expectations (which are remarkably similar in featuring love for the Cosmic Creator and their fellow human beings). If God is "above all, through all, and within all", as Jesuits believe, Christians must respect God's presence in other faith communities. Those who cannot wait in expectancy, who insist faith is knowledge, may feel no qualms about imposing their beliefs on others."

***

"A person – plus God – can be somebody!"

Rev. Bruce a black postal worker and Baptist preacher shouts at the top of his voice, sweat pouring down his face **"A person -plus God - can be somebody!"** The words punctuate his rambling sermon over and over until finally the ancient promise of deliverance touches the weary hearts of his congregation and the small church echoes with sobs, laughter and clapping...

"Praise God!"
"Thank you Jesus!"
"Amen brother."
"Thank you Jesus, thank you Lord."
"Amen, brother. Amen.."
as tears stream down the radiant faces of God's blessed poor.

**

Prayer is the gift that outlast all distractions.

**

"Who's Rev. Bruce?"

A black minister who invited Quaker-led work camps for high school and college students to stay in his church over the weekend while they worked with neighbors on Saturday painting their shabby apartments with paint supplied by the landlords.

"Why the emphasize on being somebody? I thought we were to approach God in a humble fashion; to decrease while God increased. Isn't the good reverend encouraging pride?"

Marcus Borg talks about three ways God offers salvation in scripture. To some like the Jews in Egypt and Rev. Bruce's flock, God offers liberation from bondage. To some like the Jews exiled in Babylon longing to return home, and restless post-modern souls, God offers a coming home from exile; To some like King David, Mary Magdalene, and other sinners God offers deliverance from sin. To all three God offers salvation. Pride in the first instance is essential to inspire courage in those beaten down because they are different in some way from those who shape the values of society. Pride in the second case is often used by the faith community as a way of identifying troublemakers in their midst, many of whom are genuinely seeking a deeper faith that might enrich the existing community. In the third instance pride is the cardinal sin of the ego-SELF, putting one's own interests ahead of love for God and others.

It's critical not to confuse the three ways God offers salvation: through liberation from bondage, return from exile, and deliverance from sin, so that rich people don't tell poor people to give up their pushy ways and that churches not discourage restless seekers. Or that liberals for that matter, not ignore personal sins in favor of environmental factors.

"How can we tell which group we're in?"

You'll know. After I knocked out my friend's four front teeth I didn't call it sin but I knew I'd done something terribly wrong. Many like George Fox who hadn't done anything wrong still feel they're lost in the wastelands searching for a way out, and some like Moses and Dr. King found their path to God working for social justice for their oppressed sisters and brothers.

Once we have a sense which path we're on we have to resist the encroaching influence of the other two paths. If we're in bondage to societal oppression we must not allow our cries for justice, for ourselves and our sisters and brothers, to be trivialized. We must be bold in defense of the weak and powerless. If we're seeking our way out of the wastelands of addiction, depression, or meaninglessness we don't need to beat ourselves up for not being "normal" nor turn from our path to respond to some pressing social crisis. And finally when we labor under the weight of our own wrong doing, our own sin, we must not excuse ourselves with references to our spiritual quest, or our treatment at the hands of others. We should be clear that "pride" and other compelling words like "love", "freedom", and "justice" have different shades of meaning in different segments of society, and use the key words thoughtfully to assist us on our particular journey.

"Don't the three paths overlap?"

Of course. Acknowledging my sin in hitting Kitteridge led to the search to believe in something beyond the emptiness of the cultural deities I was being offered. Later, after I was convinced of God's reality, I was led to recognize my role in perpetuating the injustices of our society; my part in constricting the liberation of others. Many of us wrestle with the demands of all three areas.

"Sounds complicated. Sorting out the different demands. And difficult. Discerning which path we're on at any given time, so we don't wander off."

Fortunately God gives us a relatively long life to allow us to attend to one concern at a time. Merton, for example, was a monk primarily concerned for individual salvation and contemplation for years before the struggle for racial justice and peace in Vietnam drew him to consider the mechanics of oppression more closely. Dorothy Day, on the other hand, identified with the struggles of the workers and poor long before she needed to replenish her inner resources with spiritual retreats and contemplative prayer. Since we are to yield all our faculties, to God the way this occurs seems a secondary and individual matter. Eventually we must return all aspects of our nature to the care of the One who formed us.

"Where'd you find that in the bible?"

The Holy One lures us through our varied faculties: our emotions, our intellect, our imagination, our fears and hopes, our intuitive grasp of reality so that we may 'love God with all our heart, soul, mind and will.'

***

Evangelism, a second look.

Years ago, shortly after I'd been energized by the Holy Spirit, a friend came to me in turmoil; unable to hold a job, to maintain a romantic relationship, his life was falling apart. After several meetings he expressed a wish to become a Christian so I prayed over him to accept Christ as his savior and receive the Holy Spirit. Later it became clear that he felt out of place in the various churches he visited and today he's married with four kids, works as a carpenter, and is a respected TM (Transcendental Meditation) instructor. I still share my Christian faith with others but I'm more appreciative of the varied ways the Spirit works in individual lives.

***

"Religion is the language of the inner landscape."
Bill Tabor. A weighty Friend at 160 pounds.

***

Willing and Knowing. Some philosophers, religious and non-religious, begin with willing rather than knowing: Augustine, Nietzsche, Sartre, and Kierkegaard. Religious philosophers, (theologians like Augustine) choose God in order to know God. Their response to the question of God's existence is to choose God sight unseen, just as one goes on a blind date purely on the suggestion of friends. Others ask around and gather information beforehand. Aristotle, Aquinas, and Pannenberg lead us through reason and logic before bringing us to God. Grace builds on nature.

***

Some believers come to God via a riveting personal encounter. Others like Cardinal Newman come to equal certitude by way of the convergence of probabilities: historical, biblical, scientific, and personal. And still others, "cradle Christians", were always at home within the Divine Milieu. Our loving God it seems reaches out to each individual in a way suited to his or her personality: thoughtful, emotional, risk-taking, conventional etc.

***

If will and intellect fail to bring us closer to God, we might look at the world around us as a painting, able like Rembrandt's self-portraits, or Cezanne's *Great Bathers* in Philadelphia to evoke the unseen radiant reality behind our natural environment. Letting the soul float free at the sight of Sandhill cranes rising from the meadow a few blocks from our home in Albuquerque, or gulls, walking rather awkwardly on the beach before soaring in the wide sky above I'm overcome with wonder at the Creator behind the creation. *Le Beau Dieu*, The Beautiful God visible in the beauty around us.

> *…Praise God you quarks*
> *cavorting herky jerky twos and threes*
> *dancing to your atomic destinies.*

> *Praise God you macromolecules of DNA*
> *endlessly breeding a billion thees and mes and more*
> *to outlive wars into eternity.*
> *Praise God for consistencies*
> *to sustain us while we wait upon deliverance;*
> *for the unborn lamb wombwarm within to wake.*

CHAPTER 5

JESUS

·····────◆────·····

We speak of Jesus as a primal word. We make a clearing in the forest of words for the Word who was flesh. We leave God and Love to one side to walk into the mystery of a new primal word. Jesus is not a memory. He's not what happened a long time ago. He comes from the future into our daily lives, or he doesn't come at all. Let the dead bury the dead.

"But you believe Jesus was raised from the dead. You experienced that in your own life. Your faith depends on a prior experience."

I can't give myself to a past experience; to a frozen belief. I can only give myself to what is present to me right now. I treasure my conversion, but I can't let it stand in to fight my battles today. I need the living Jesus. The one still risen. The one who is here with me in the clutter around us. Every day I live farther and farther away from my first experience. Every day other experiences modify my original encounter. So every day I need the Lord's presence in my life. All the way through to the end of my time on earth. It's too easy to rest on a few wonderful experiences. A few core beliefs. But Jesus is still with us today. Still calling us to join him in working for the Kingdom of God on earth. First conversion, enlightenment, or convincement; then we're put to work. Regardless of our creed, color, or sexual orientation.

"I think you're making a mistake."

Not the Manger

Our beginning is not the manger
cross
or tomb
but Emmaus where eyes grew wide

Early apostle put out her hand
to touch the corpse
"Rabbani!"
"Mary"
ran to tell good news.

PaulknockedIbelieveit fromblessedhorseblinded.

Crowd in the room bewildered by rumor. Can it be?'
Caesar's road law and language spiders every
damn acre. Can it be? Imean look?
Look at the ma n stan ding ther e can itbe! Yesheartstspounding yes
as warm riverlets parted the dust on tanned faces
and o my God how heart's laughter flowed.

As they grew calmer
took a deep breath to settle
they no longer exclaimed "Can it be?"

Spirit sang in the bloodstream
holding them to the great work ahead.

***

Jesus, for the purposes of this work is not God. As a primal word Jesus is associated with but not identified with Love and God. Like other primal words Jesus has his own unique identity.

Jesus up close from a distance.

Keeping the focus on Jesus we back away
from questions on Jesus and his relationship to
evil
Paul
women
On Jesus!
Modern psychology
Fundamentalists and apocalyptic cults
On Jesus!
Scars from Sunday school or nuns or whatever
horrific incidents
Drove us from the church
On Jesus!
U.F.O.'s, reincarnation, the sexual revolution
On Jesus!
Environmental issues, near death experiences
On Jesus!
World religions, crystals and mantras
On Jesus!
Nuclear weapons, national elections, and war
On Jesus!

Black holes, quasars, quarks, and the expanding
universe
On Jesus!
Biblical scholarship, death and the afterlife
On Jesus!

***

That a man had been raised from the dead was thought by the vast majority of educated Romans in the first century common time to be sheer foolishness. No one needed the Enlightenment, or modem science, to dismiss such rumors as contrary to common sense. Sheer foolishness..

***

When T.S. Eliot became a Christian in his late thirties his friends were dismayed. "Poor dear Tom Eliot..." Virginia Woolfe said, "May be called dead to us all from this day forward. There's something obscene about a living person sitting by the fire and believing in God."

***

"Where there is mystery there must be faith. Faith you cannot change. No matter how you look at it either you have it, or you don't."

Mother Teresa

"When a reporter asked Mother Teresa 'What made you start your work, what inspired you and kept you going during so many years?' and Mother Teresa answered, 'We do it all for Jesus' the reporter looked disappointed. Her response has become her watchword, the explanation she gives for the activity and success of the sisters, 'we do it for Jesus; everything. All the time.'"

Edward LeJoly,
Mother Teresa of Calcutta

***

Kneeling by my cot in prayer on a weekend retreat from the Army in Gethsemane monastery in Kentucky in my early twenties, I was startled by the words... "Betty, my wife."... And she has been ever since.

***

Lord, interrupt my expectations. Press through my fears. Be with me in any way you wish.

***

Good afternoon... Lord? So many inner guests crowd for attention smiling, "Just a word", gesturing with a wave or change of expression. Which one is you?

***

"Your presentational methods make me uncomfortable. I wonder if you're not expecting too much from the reader. It's not that I'm not moved. HELP!"

***

People who lump all Christians together; who can't distinguish between Mother Teresa and Dr. King and rightwing homophobic Evangelicals are in need of remedial assistance before they're permitted to engage in civilized discourse. Dr Bill Johnson my irascible black neighbor is such person. He lumps all Christians together, black and white, all religions for that matter, hating them all for the horrors experienced in the south during his childhood.

He despises them all. "You can't know the rage that flames out from me. The insults I've suffered in my lifetime from good white Christians." I defend your presence Lord pointing to Dr. King, Bishop Tutu and our daughters Wendy and Chris who've spent their working lives as social workers advocating for the disabilitied (Wendy) and refugees from Latin America (Chris), but the issue is far from resolved.

Bill teaches chemistry at Penn and is dying of cancer. He still pickets every week as he has for forty years, on behalf of black people, underpaid workers, women, and environmental issues. Perhaps I'm in need of remedial assistance before I can converse with those Christianity has abused. Perhaps I'm living among flames like the rich man separated from the blessed poor.

***

If you want to find Jesus go to Christians whom you admire on other grounds.

"What do you mean by 'on other grounds?'"

The people whom you'd admire even if they weren't Christians. Religion has always been about separating sheep from goats. True prophets from false. Amos, Jeremiah, and Isiah separated faithful Jews from unfaithful Jews. Jesus, Luther, and Dr. King in our day, were cracks of lightning that lit up a murky landscape exposing the darker motivations at work behind the religious facade. If we want to hear Christianity's primal word we can't avoid controversy. We must listen for the presence of Christ, not only in faith communities, but also among the conflicting prophecy of contentious factions, putting to one side the less authentic voices to adhere to the voice of love speaking to the world today.

***

Perhaps we need a periodic repopulation of Dante's inferno with contemporary religious figures who have betrayed their trust.

A visible distinction between the false prophets who outnumbered the true prophets forty - or was it four hundred? - To one.

True prophets flourish - not quite the exact word - are revealed? By the enemies they make. Making the right enemies is more important than making the right friends. Friends give you love and support; enemies challenge you to change the world.

Border Patrol

Scripture tells us God is loveand yet
Jesus whipped the money-changers out of the Temple.
Why were Amos and Jeremiah mad?
Why were Miss Day, Camus and Rabbi Hecshel who
despite a life of service to the least
flint-faced and unforgiving?

What set saints apart from wife abusers, demagogues
and more enlightened folk
who let off steam to integrate their anger,
complete their personalities?

Hearing homily on Christ the King
after Matthew 25
had separated sheep
from those who would ignore the least
I waited for the shift
that all too often softened sermons in our suburban
sanctuary;

but halfway through
AIDs and homelessness
evoked the vast impenetrable continent of discontent

that lay beyond our fortified frontier
and I saw the saints standing on the border
eyes rimmed with tears of rage
pointing to the wretched kin we had ignored
wrotha
and I was visited by a unseen Sunfire in our midst
that will not subside
until the continent un-bordered lies
beneath God's wide and penetrating gaze
and every single tear is dry.

***

Like a nervous homilist I live in fear of losing your attention; but then again like a mischievous child I'm always interrupting my own sermon.

***

Jesus Among the Media

Blessed are the poor. [Jesus quotes from Matthew 5:3-11 NRSV]
Rabbi?
Yes.
Some question your concern for the poor. You've been quoted as saying they will always be with us. That poverty is inevitable; without remedy. People also say your campaign for the disadvantaged is being financed, behind the scenes, by certain wealthy women. You've been seen eating and drinking freely at lavish banquets. Would you care to comment?"
Blessed are those who mourn, *for they...*

At one party you encouraged women of questionable reputation to bathe you in expensive perfumes. Is this the message you want to send on caring for the less fortunate?

Blessed are the meek, for...

You've counselled turning the other cheek to our enemies. While no one is saying that you, personally, are not a brave man, such a passive response to Roman oppression is seen as cowardly, even traitorous. How do you respond to these charges?

Blessed are those who hunger and thirst for righteousness, for they will...

Some say the long nights of prayer in the hills have affected your mental stability. That you imagine yourself some sort of God. What evidence can you offer that you are not, in fact, suffering from delusions of grandeur? Or perhaps a psychotic disorder brought on by a birth trauma, about which there have been rumors?

Blessed are the merciful, for...

Neighbors from Nazareth say you are unfeeling and harsh. That you have rejected your own family and closest friends. That you focus attention on yourself, rather than on God and God's Law. That you are tearing apart the fabric of family and civil life. Your response?

Blessed are the pure in heart...

There have been rumors that you visit prostitutes. That you are, in fact, currently having an affair with a woman from Magdalene. Do you deny? These allegations?

*Blessed are the peacemakers, for them...*You've been called a demagogue, a dangerous extremist, who wishes to overthrow the government and set up his own kingdom.

Blessed are those who are persecuted for righteousness sake for theirs is the kingdom of heaven.

"Many say this kingdom of yours is a diversion from the real problems facing the nation. They say it is compassionate folly; that caring for that disadvantaged will raise taxes and stifle individual initiative; that turning the other cheek is cowardly and leaves our women and children defenseless. Would you care to comment?

Blessed are you when people revile you and persecute you and utter all kinds of evil against you falsely on..."

Are you suggesting you haven't been given a fair opportunity to express your views to the public? That there is a conspiracy, by the media, to misrepresent your views? Would you care to comment on the nature of this conspiracy? And how it relates to the messianic rumors swirling around your movement?

***

Christian Sociology

Jesus never talks about the middle class. When Betty and I were in a Quaker work camp in a poor Mexican village a campesino told me I was rich. I protested I had just married and had a low level job back home working for subsistence pay for the Quakers.

"No, no, senor. You are rich. You have shoes." He and the other villagers wore sandals cut from old tires.

***

Who suffered most from the death of Jesus?

His mother weeping, watching her favorite son sagging on a bloody cross above the small gathering? John beside her under the cross? The women? His followers scattered in Jerusalem and Galilee? Francis pierced by fiery nails on a mountain in Tuscany? Catherine pierced in Sienna? The poor, the wretched, the least in our wealthy world? Well aren't we? You and I and all our friends? Don't we have shoes? The Son himself, gasping for air, nailed to hard fresh wood?

Or God in heaven, Father, Mother, loving parent, who watched iron spikes hammered into wood through your son's wrists as Jesus lay on the cross; and then hammered through the ankles till Jesus was ready to be lifted up into the parched sky. Then the iron barb thrust between the ribs. The sharp pointed thorns tearing the flesh, scrapping the skull of God's first born son, while below the soldiers gloated and were pleased Herod was standing firm against the rebellious Jews.

You know what I'm saying? God suffers. Dying or watching God suffers. Disgraced. Humiliated. A convicted criminal, between two thieves. Spit on, jeered and mocked. Deserted by friends.

Ok that's not what makes sense in today's world is it? But how can I not weep when my beloved friend, my savior, dies? As the evil one gloats. But leave Satan aside. Jesus has been crucified; my friend has died. And the tears come. I would not bypass the wretched poor in whom God still suffers. But I weep because if Jesus did not die in the exact way I have described it, God did not suffer. And if God did not suffer we worship a pasteboard God, stuck up on a church wall. A picture, a statue, an idol conceived by human aspiration. An omnipotent abstraction. Because no one could have conceived of a God who ate, digested, and eliminated food. Who was hauled up a hill by rough soldiers and nailed to two beams of wood. But if Jesus died in the exact way I have recorded, then God is love.

Not risen love. Not miraculous love come back from the tomb. But first, just love, love by itself alone. Just plain garden variety love for one's friends. Whether it's clear that God is almighty, come back from the grave; or is powerless, left to the earth's corruption, it is clear that God is love.

On Friday, hanging on the cross under the blazing sun, God is love. On Saturday, lying rigid and lifeless in the cave, God is love. On Sunday, getting up early to go and speak to Mary Magdalene, God is love.

Think of this. Jesus, our friend who lived with us, and talked with us, and sat at table with us; who healed us; who touched our flesh and said, "Be well", who taught us to seek the shy kingdom of love that emerges among us, who called us to turn from SELF to serve him in our sisters and brothers. Think of this Jesus. Generous, open-hearted, forgiving us over and over and over, even the worst of us, even and especially the lost hateful sheep, the very worst of us. Then think of your worst enemy, of humankind's worst enemy. The one you cannot stand. That is the human being for whom Christ died. Not the good people, but the sinners. The worst among us because whatever else God may be, first, last and forever God is love.

Jesus Over Water

Jesus! Jesus! Over water.

"Leave your little boast for me. Come and see.
See my sanity amid what seems the ebb and fantasy
of flight from world I willed you.
Come and see.
Out over choppy water I
would greet you.

Leave your little boast.
Give it to me.

I will hold and - don't slip!
Keep your eyes on me!
I come. I see you struggling there
I know I care.
Clinging to the gunnel clutching side
can't you see my seas capsize your crafty ways?
I had you in mind not all John.
Leave that crowd behind I want to talk to you my
child.
You thought I did not know?
Gulls over bay. I did not care?
Rag monkey came from me.
I was the one clutched to your side looking
for warm light across the bay.
I was the lighted window.
I was the family inside sitting down to dinner
We had a place for you
set aside.

Come. Come across the water. Come to me.
Daddy's hug waits on the other side.

Mary. "Where'd that come from?"

My dad left me on my fifth birthday and I didn't hear from him again till I was seventeen.

***

Visions. I see a huge black bear standing up outside the kitchen window. It leaps through the window, shattering glass flying everywhere... An immense wave curls toward the unprotected beach... the distant crack in the icy Artic landscape alerts my mind to a change in the awesome stillness... the SUNFIRE on Walnut Street...

***

Hiking in the Alps two days after the Louvre. Staring up the icy slopes dwarfed by the towering slabs of rock and white gleaming peaks... "This is my art. This is the way I paint."

***

Twenty years ago driving home from a charismatic prayer meeting at St. Anastasia... "I want you to become a Catholic."...

***

Means of Grace. Scripture, creeds, rosaries and other devotional activities which point in the direction of Jesus will all pass. Even the sacraments, Catholics believe, will pass. These go-betweens, these little intermediaries, without the invisible God at one end, and tangible human beings at the other are lifeless. They're like a bridge suspended over water that fails to connect two bodies of land. Even should one end of the bridge be grounded in God's very presence, unless it leads to at least one human being the bridge is useless. Even should every Christian, every human being on earth walk across the bridge unless it leads to the living God, the bridge again is suspended over empty water.

> No liturgy without participants
> No scripture without readers
> No beliefs without believers

Scripture will fade, sacraments will come to an end, and the creeds will pass. Only God and God's people will endure. Therefore value people over beliefs, creeds, scriptures and churchy paraphernalia.

NEVERTHELESS TREASURE your collection of beliefs and practices as a mountain climber treasures her spiked boots, her thermal clothing and the life rope that webs her to her companions. Treasure the map that guides you to the summit, while others share theirs, for who can say from the valley floor merging with the long slopes yearning for the radiant summit which map, which set of climbing gear, which team strategy may prove more useful?

The mountain is vast and dangerous enough to allow for a variety of approaches without bickering over the one true map, the one true path to the top.

***

"Everything that rises must converge."

Flannery O'Connor

***

My First Annual Conference. Separated from my friends from the prayer community on the boardwalk in Atlantic City, feeling lost among thousands of Catholic charismatic strangers I heard the inner Voice say "Aren't I enough?"

So many times since, discouraged and alone, those words come back "Aren't I enough?" It always makes me smile and often laugh..

***

The primal word may be spoken in one word; believers' "Lord", my "Betty", Joseph Conrad's "Horror" or in several words: marriage vows, the 23rd psalm, orders given to inflict violence on one's fellow human beings.. The primal word is revealed in its expression and remains secluded. Is fully given... and withheld. The scent of wine that lingers in the dusty glass intoxicates the thirsting soul.

***

What we need is not more talk about infallible truth but a companion for the journey.

"Are you suggesting Jesus is not the infallible truth? Is not God? Didn't Christ say, 'I am the truth' as well as 'I am the way?' Doesn't his being the compassionate companion depend on his being more than human? More than an example, a model, a teacher? On his being in fact the infallible truth?"

Paul Ricoeur talks…

"Paul who?"

Ricoeur. A postmodern French hermeneutist and phenomenologist who…

"Forget the who."

Riceour says creedal truth claims emerge from biblical language, from "stories prophecies, laws, hymns and so forth". If we abstract from this lived level of human experience a few creedal statements we miss the God who led the Jews out of bondage in Egypt, back from exile in Babylon; who prophesied the coming Messiah; and who, for Christians, was God's Son Jesus, born from Mary's womb in a stable when Joseph and Mary were turned away from the inn, and who spent the last three years of his life healing, teaching, and gathering disciples to spread the good news of the coming kingdom of God. We miss the outpourings of the psalmist, the inner Voice that spoke to Sarah, Abraham and the prophets, the wrestlings of Job, and the sad wisdom of the Preacher. The tenderness of the *Song of Songs* where the Divine Nature woos, courts, enraptures the human soul. If God had wanted to present only infallible Truth to humanity surely the bible, with its varied theological perspectives (tribal warrior deity, cosmic creator and fearful judge, sacrificial loving savior, etc.) and its four varied accounts of the life of Jesus would have to be severely edited. Or placed in an appendix to the one definitive theology. One slim brochure of faith and practice, even a couple of pages, should encompass the theological requirements of the believing community.

"You haven't answered my question. Is Jesus the infallible truth?"

Of course, but that's just the beginning.

***

If Jesus is the infallible truth why are the creeds and most theology based on Paul and not the life and words of Jesus?

***

Walking by the Tanguy pond in 1982… "I love you as much as I love my son, Jesus."

***

"Widen the fibers of my being that I may absorb more of your love."

A once Quaker now Catholic friend and contemplative

***

"Could we take a break here? To give the readers a chance to collect themselves, use the facilities, whatever, before our next big push. To give us a break."

Us?

"Inner voices get tired too."

Just before her annual trip from Atlantic City to Palm Beach in the big white Cadillac mother asked me to pray for her eyesight. The eye doctor had told her not to drive, but she insisted so I held her hands and prayed a short prayer in the name of Jesus for a safe journey. A week later she called from Palm Beach to say her eyesight had improved remarkably. And that her ophthalmologist had no explanation for her blurry vision being in remission.

***

For over a year I'd been wrestling with the competing claims of the major world religions. Sitting alone in Francis's dim chapel at St. Damien in Assisi the words unexpectedly came that ended my search allowing the long poem to go forward.

Twelve Gates to the City

"Those passing through twelve gates
will meet the God who is not other than they have known.
In that Light
infinitely more than anything that they have known
all find themselves one family."

Breathing prayer

Jeeee/susssss

IIIIII/lonnnng

Toooo/ seeeee

Yourrrr/ faaaace

Aaaa/ ginnnnn

Stillness

Sitting quietly alone; twenty, thirty, sixty minutes at a time until silence settles into stillness where two spirits share one space. Or sometimes we talk. It all depends.

"Sixty minutes?"

In the beginning or on retreat.

"On retreat?"

Only an hour at a time, and no more than three hours a day.

"But only ten minutes?"

As I get older I seem to tap into stillness quite quickly. And the *Jesus Journal* where we converse in writing usually twice a day probably helps. The Spirit speaks to others according to their need and nature.

***

Quietly circling the interior of Holy Rosary, a new, creamy white, softly molded adobe style palace of worship in Albuquerque the day before Easter, I was surprised by the Lord's words *"See what my people have built for me?"* The next day at mass in the crowded church the Voice spoke again. *"See how my people love me? How they sing my praises? How they honor my name?"* And I was thrilled to sense the Lord's approval of our poor efforts to please the Most High God.

Scenic Detour

Personal Journey from Devotional Faith to Socratic Symposium

"Looks a bit long for general consumption, John."

Reader beware. The shorter bits pick up again after later again after five and a half pages.

Excluded from the humanistic philosophic terrain occupied by the neo-Logical Positivists, Nietzsche, Marx, Freud and the scientific milieu of the late 20th century I retreated during my middle years to a monastic enclave in a secluded wood. There I visited with the intellectually quaint Christian contemplatives:

Meister Eckhart, Julian of Norwich, Teresa of Avila, John of the Cross, Boehme, George Fox and Jan von Ruysbroek. And then, wonder of wonders, five years ago I began reading philosophy again.

As I read I realized that though I'd given up too much disputable territory to a post-modern mentality I could no longer return to my devotional clearing in the wood. Athenian robes and medieval garb no longer fit. The modern Christian thinkers I valued especially Kierkegaard and Dostoevsky perceptively explored the subjective side of Christian experience while Karl Barth and C.S. Lewis restated the traditional objective truth claims but neither groups was able to my satisfaction to convey the breath of understanding that absorbed and then moved beyond the modern and post-modern mid-set. Often insightful and passionate, they repeated the devotional theological concerns of the Christian enclave I wished to widen.

Determined to remain within the general parameters of the humanistic landscape around me I resonated to Wittgenstein's "language games" which challenged the right of any one body of thought to speak for the varied sub-groups of which contemporary society is composed. Christianity, along with other religions and ideologies, had as much right to its interpretation of reality - to Truth - as the empiricists and other advocates of a one-dimensional reality. Language games allowed for varied ideological and religious enclaves to conduct meaningful activities among themselves, and engage the wider society in issues of the common good, the meaningful life, and justice for the poor and marginalized. While Wittgenstein established the right of Christians to have their language, faith, and practices respected, he left open the question of how Christians might engage others in meaningful dialogue.

Still feeling isolated I stumbled upon the reigning European liberal political thinker Jurgen Habermas' "discourse ethics" which provided strategies for meaningful communication between adversaries. Though tailored to emancipatory movements in dialogue with oppressive forces in the wider culture (labor/management, racial and ethnic minorities vs. the status quo etc.) discourse ethics and Wittgenstein's language games allowed Christians to discuss and work together to resolve common problems. Perhaps Christians in the manner of Haberman, Socrates, and the Talmudic rabbis might engage with Buddhists, scientists, and humanists – with whoever. Perhaps the news I perceived as good might be shared in the marketplace of contending ideas.

Grateful for Wittgenstein's "language games" and Habermas' "discourse ethics" I still missed a visceral sense of where I, or any believer Christian or not, fit in to the contemporary discussion on the major ethical, political, and aesthetic issues. I knew of course my participation was welcome provided I left my faith outside. Then Hans-George Gadamer, another humanistic European philosopher came to my rescue. Gadamer's point-of-view hermeneutics ("the art or science of interpretation") which established the right of each participant to speak from her or his own orientating truth – what Gadamer called "prejudices" – brought another dimension to the search for a seat at the table. He exposed the unconscious motivations, and personal biases that animated each participant, grounding the discussion not only in meaningful intellectual communication, but allowing for passionate personal components to be become involved as well. If I spoke out of a particular bias, Gadamer implied, so did non-Christians. Rather than feeling defensive that my position was unverifiable in scientific terms, I began to see that other positions were also based· on underlying intuitive (not necessarily irrational) assumptions. On what Gadamer called "prejudices." To make the fact that a participant had *not* had a religious experience the basis for a comprehensive truth claim binding on others seemed rather arbitrary. I've not been to China, but I would not deny its existence, or interpret my lack of experience in ways that contradicted eye witness accounts,

Moving on from Wittgenstein.

Moving on from Wittgenstein's language games, through Habermas's discourse ethics to Gadamer's point of view hermeneutics I felt ready to enter the late 20th century fray of contending ideas and ideologies. I felt empowered to venture beyond my devotional enclave to claim the wider philosophic terrain around me in the name of the sovereign God, whose land I felt had been usurped by alien - well not quite alien, perhaps limited? Constricted? - Forces. What an undertaking faced me! I was eager to begin.

Before presenting the case for Christianity however, two initial pitfalls must be identified. First, we must not, like Karl Barth and many evangelicals merely restate the main events of Christian revelation: Creation, fall, Incarnation, etc. on a take it or leave it basis. Useful in nurturing the believing community itself, especially when it wanders from its core beliefs such an approach can be off-putting to others. It may fail to engage them in fruitful dialogue as Paul did with philosophers in Athens, becoming all things to all people in order to witness to the risen Christ. On the other hand we mustn't modify or discard the main tenets of Christian faith to fit contemporary needs.

Because Jesus is one of our most influential cultural ikons conservatives and liberals often utilize Christ's teachings to promote their own agendas. While not questioning God's presence in either tradition we must not allow their political agendas to become the main focus of attention, while Jesus becomes the justifying agent – the front man – for decisions reached on other grounds.

John?

I know Lord. Which is not to deny you speak through those concerned for justice and mercy whatever their beliefs.

Move on.

Another dilemma we face is how do we approach the truth claims themselves? Are we to ignore the tradition out of which the truth faith claims emerged to challenge the unconverted with direct questions, "Do you believe in God? In the Resurrection? Have you accepted Jesus as your personal savior?" Or are we to approach the claims in the way scripture would suggest i.e. -through the narratives, prophecies, hymns, visionary revelations, and historical accounts that the bible presents as the milieu in which previous seekers from Abraham and Sarah to the Johannine community made their faith commitments? Framing Christian beliefs as philosophical truth claims separating them from their natural setting in scripture and the on-going Judeo-Christian tradition raises them to the level of intellectual questions apart from the experience of the faith community.

On the other hand allowing Christian truth claims to be interpreted solely by the heroic history, creeds, sacraments, and life style of a particular denomination: Catholic, Baptist, Mennonite etc. narrows the dialogue to…

"John? Let me see if I'm following your argument. Are you suggesting Christian truth claims be placed in their biblical setting without undue denominational influence?"

Not quite. I'm suggesting pondering truth claims is only one of the possible first steps leading to an individual's relationship with Christ. Even if it's a step forward it's not the final step. After one has wrestled with the extraordinary claims of traditional

Christianity: that Jesus was the Son of God, was God, was crucified, and was preserved from corruption to rise from…

And so on,

One is drawn into a closer relationship with this iconic figure who appears in the narratives, parables, prophecies and hymns in the Judeo-Christian tradition. And no authority: Paul, or Luther, or Mother Teresa may decisively modify one's relation to Jesus.

For some Jesus is a guiding and comforting presence, for others an inner auditory voice of love. For still others Jesus appears in his transformed flesh calling them to "Follow me." Seventeen times in the New Testament Jesus calls an individual to "Follow me." Follow him where? Into verbal assent to the crucifixion and resurrection and other stables of Christian belief. Or to follow Jesus in adhering to his teaching which can lead to persecution and even martyrdom? For some like Francis of Assisi yes; for others "Follow Me "means to listen to the inner Christ as one's life unfolds. The danger of the first option is one may…

John. Move on.

Belief and membership are not enough. And for many even discipleship is not enough. Teresa of Avila, foundress of Carmelite communities all over Spain often said "send me no sad sisters". To love God is to be filled with joy. Touched by the primal word Jesus one babbles words of thanksgiving and praise. One is lifted into…

"Why must you wander away from the discussion at hand into these ecstatic babblings? First you argue quietly for the role of Jesus as a viable option for the modem seeker. Then you turn up the volume to proselytize emotionally for an aging and discredited religiosity."

I'm not trying to recruit souls for Christ but I *am* constrained to witness to the truth I have been given. What anyone makes of my witness is their own affair. I admit my witness is not to a merely personal experience, but to that experience as it confirms the central claims of the gospel.

"How do you reconcile the reason-based viable option approach with the devotional intensity associated with the primal word?"

I agree. It *is* a leap from the acceptance of Christianity's propositional truth claims to the experience of the living God in Jesus Christ, God's son. A leap from those who accepted the baptism of John; who knew the things of God with their head (the Incarnation, the Resurrection and so on) to the baptism of the Holy Spirit, who conveys the things of God to the heart is a stretch. I don't think this gap between knowledge and inner experience is accidental. There are several passages in *Acts*, I can't recall now, that speak of the gift of the Holy Spirit as distinct from most believer's commitment to the creeds and teaching of their denomination. I think it's part of the process of our on-going salvation; a way to enlist all our faculties: emotions, intuition and deeper spirit, as well as our intellectual assent. So that we love God with all our heart, soul and mind as the bible says.

"But you would not deny the possibility that others may resonate to primal words that do not echo the presence of Jesus?"

Of course. I can only share what I've been given. Others will speak from their own understanding.

102 End of Scenic Detour

Sweet Assassin

Languidly embraced by an overstuffed chair
listening to Guardini's Lord
sermon-scented Sundays echo faintly
until I sense I am not coveted;

set round with slivers of tribal doctrine rising like
a fence
I must elude
to roam wild meadows
of my unexplode late adolescent life.

Guardini parrots not the Christian choir
clammering for my immortal soul.
Pearl he prizes glows not incessantly
lazering unassailable light into recesses of my hesitant
soul.
Glimmers shyly... "Would you?"

Words slip in under armor piercing like a thin dagger
wobbly entrails of accumulated wisdom.
Then of course you were there. In white
Gleaming I suppose
soliciting my life and I said yes
heart pounding yes Lord yes.

***

JESUS 2

Jesus Among the Masses

Fresh from the Incarnation
the King of Glory slipped unnoticed in among the
masses as a carpenter
and later gardener to Mary Magdalene
beggar beside Martin of Tours high upon his
horse
leper to Francis & Damien
garbage men to Dr. King
street people to Dorothy Day
pedestrians to Merton in Louisville
the poorest of the Calcutta's poor to Mother's
nuns
daily pilgrims knocking at the Benedictine door,
old people to my poet friend Shelia Roberts.

That of God in every person to my Quaker Friends.

Keep your eyes open! You never know. Especially among the poor.'

***

When Alice, Nell's neighbor, died at Dunwoody I told a cleaning lady who was weeping outside Alice's door that "Jesus will take care of her." I would not have said that to Nell, my mother-in-law, or other residents, but I assumed without thinking, that a poor woman would understand. Where else had she to go?

For the rich, with our basic needs met, God is an option available depending on one's interest and temperament, but the poor will always turn to God, for they have nowhere else to go.

***

Hesitation

Surrounded by established voices
the Psalmist
Dante
Hopkins,
Eliot;
one hesitates to expose one's own flawed gift
among so many whose voices ring clear and bold
across the frozen meadow
choiring in the new born king.

One hesitates
but one does not hold back.

***

Dream The lights are out and as we walk I say to my companion, referring to a young black man we'd met earlier, "Us drunks are cheerful on the middle slopes."

***

Toward the end of my first counseling with Marie Gatza as I lay on the cot at Ghost Ranch, New Mexico, sobbing for my lost dad, the little Jewish girl on the beach, Kitt'ridge grinning at me through his missing front teeth, and the red-haired boy's head bouncing off the concrete steps words of relief came. "I bore your wounds, I open your wounds, I heal your wounds." That's why we call him Savior.

***

I can't image what it means that God suffers for the whole "groaning creation", but I know I'm part of God's healing. I know God uses us "wounded healers" to help others.

***.

"Between hope and absolute knowledge we have
to choose. We cannot have both."
                                                    Paul Riceour

***

Flashback. Sensing I was coming to the end of our second nine month counseling session Dr.Marie Gatza suggested I go on a Passion Week retreat at Wernersville, the *Jesuit Spiritual Center* in rural Pennsylvania. On the final day, Monday after Easter, I experienced a life-changing exchange of love offerings. During the third hour of prayer I offered my hidden heart to God, the place of openness that is accessible only in stillness. The pain and uncertainty were extreme. Not a physical but a heart pain as if one were stretching one's soul in the offering. In uncertainty. Not knowing if this was presumptuous or not; a reaching for spiritual favors beyond one's leading. There was no guide for I was asking the guide himself to respond to my offering. My whole soul cried out for God's substantial presence.

Neither encouraged nor discouraged I made my deepest being available until I heard you Lord Say I was to widen my heart to receive your love. Then I sensed I was to wait. I had made my offering and I was to wait on God to respond to my need; relief from the pain of separation, of inner deprivation. After lunch kneeling before the tabernacle in the dim baroque three story indoor chapel I heard the words, *"I give you the whole world to fill your heart. Look for my love in the events of your life."*

It was over. I'd come to the end of a difficult counseling and was being sent back into the world with these puzzling words. For years I'd been led to find God apart from the world's "blooming, buzzing, confusion" and now my strength was to come from the world.

"You felt as if you had been expelled from the friendly confines of your devotional life?"

Exactly. But over the next several weeks the Spirit continued to speak interpreting the inner word that the whole world would fill my heart. The old tension between inner/ outer, thinking/ feeling, prayer time/ work time, their time/ my time relaxed and I felt more intimately connected to life around me. Especially to others. Heidegger's being-alongside, being with; Marcel's intersubjectivity became...

"You were going to mention the Spirit's words that interpreted the puzzling original word."

Thank you. I was told to care for Betty and to *"Expect to meet me and my love in those around you. And in the creation; the landscape and rivers and the times of waiting... Love and embrace*

*them and they will renew you. You will find strength in embracing
my world around you. Later I will tell you about the whole world."*...

"What do you think was meant by 'the whole world' "?

I don't know. It may have something to do with another inner
word of love that came just after Wernersville... *"I want you to
write of my presence in the whole world. That I am the God of heaven
and earth, the sustainer and lover of the whole universe.*

"Is that why you returned to philosophy? To broaden your
view of the world beyond the devotional enclave?"

Sure. Counseling unearthed my slumbering intellect; my
ability to think not just feel and intuit my way through life.

"Balancing your strong F (feelings) and N (intuition) with the
resurrected T (thinking)?" Again Mary Masseuse.

Yes. The Jungian based Myers-Briggs personality test was a
great help.

***

"You said you were eager to challenge the current postmodern
world view, which you called one-dimensional, materialistic and
terminally solipsistic. Are you still eager to join the fray to claim
the philosophic landscape for the God of heaven and earth?"

John?

Yes Lord?

*Make your case but don't neglect the tension between theology
and the primal words. Jesus! God!*

***

The Hebrew notion of God as ruler of heaven and earth,
of history and science, has passed from our consciousness. I
hesitate to break the agreement Christians have made with the
prevailing humanistic world view, which allows them a certain
freedom of expression, for fear of appearing paradoxically narrow

and parochial in claiming too much in today's world for God's sovereignty. Especially after the horrors of World War II.

"Could you stay focused on Jesus, rather than God. I'm fearful of a long God theology, followed by lengthy Christian modifications."

Mary M. "My concern is that the primal word Jesus has been evoked obliquely. Without *some* truth claims, *some* theology, all the narratives, poems, paradoxes and prayers become anecdotal, a matter of individual taste, and you're back in your restricted enclave."

For four hundred years on either side of the birth of Christ Western philosophy was dominated by classical thinkers: Socrates (470 B.C.E.?), Plato, Aristotle, Plotinus, Stoics and Epicureans. For twelve hundred years from Augustine in the fifth century to Descartes in the sixteenth century Christian thought prevailed. Aquinas, Dun Scotus, and the late medieval scholastics vied among themselves over the proper relationship between the triune God and God's creation. Gradually through the Renaissance and decisively in the Enlightenment, humanistic philosophers once again set the agenda. Today with a few notable exceptions the European philosophic terrain is humanistic. The more recent heirs of Descartes, including Husserl, Heidegger, Sartre, Dewey, Derrida, Simone De Beauvoir, Hannah Arendt, Merleau-Ponty, Habermas and Gadamer focus on political, aesthetic, and metaphysical interpretations of reality, while others like Bertram Russell, E.G. Moore, Gottlob Frege, Popper and the early Wittgenstein take a more scientific and linguistic approach. On both sides of the channel, and the Atlantic, other aspects of reality are emphasized over the decisive importance of Jesus.

Religious philosophers who have focused on the risen Jesus include Kierkegaard, Karl Barth, Jurgen Moltman, Teilhard de Chardin, Karl Rahner, Gabriel Marcel, Catherine LaCugna, and

Pannenberg. For other significant theological viewpoints see the martyred Bonhoeffer, Paul Tillich, Elizabeth Johnson, Mary Daly, Marcus Borg, and John Crossman.

John.

Yes Lord.

Move on.

Summary?

Briefly.

The only point I would draw from this sparse overview of the history of philosophy is that thinking in any era is related to the prevailing political and cultural climate. That Christian thought prevailed for eight hundred years over classical thought, does not necessarily mean Christians were right and the Greeks and Romans wrong. Nor does the prevailing one-dimensional view of reality today mean that Christianity is now wrong and humanistic and scientific interpretations are the last word. The quarrel between Hegel, the consummate rationalist spanning left wing Marxism and right wing fascism, and Kierkegaard who speaks for the single individual against the surrounding culture comes to mind. Sometimes I side with Kierkegaard in his concern for the solitary individual. Sometimes with Hegel and Chardin in their concern for the broader historical struggle to bring the whole human family to unity over the divisive forces in history. As a Christian of course, de Chardin's Christ-centered evolutionary Omega Point elicits my allegiance far more than Hegel's history-bound impersonal, Spirit of thought. In their devotional lives de Chardin and Kierkegaard sit at the same fire. I just want to be part of their circle.***

Science can tell us how things work, but not why things exist at all. That question can only be asked by considering the wider context within which science operates. Jasper's calls this wider context the Comprehensive. Heidegger's being. This is the realm that philosophy has always concerned itself with. Not how does one being within Being relate to another, but how does one being, the human being, relate to the totality of existence itself?

That we, as limited, finite, parts of the wider whole can even ask such a question is simply amazing. The part questions the whole! The incomplete, the fallible, questions, considers, ponders, envisages the completeness of reality. The time worn creature whose life on earth is a blink in time's long gaze widens it's questioning eyes to the wide range between the beginning, duration, and end of human history, to the end of the universe. Widens its questioning gaze to ponder the snarled threads of evil and good until the tension between the two is clearly exposed.

***

"It seems I should pass; there's only one essay question, and it can be about anything you like."

John Ashberry

***

"Theology does not really need to retreat to subjectivism. In coherently restating the content of Christian doctrine, the discipline of systematic thought can stand on its own without a prior guarantee of truth."

Wolfhart Pannenberg

True John but not our principal area of concern. Your bits of logic float in a sea of uncertainty. Your role is to focus on primal words which brighten the cracks in traditional theology.

***

God made the world in seven days and then after the flood, the Exodus, the Covenant, exile and return, the restoration of the

Temple and five hundred years when nothing much happened Christ appears as the Son of God who died for our sins and was raised to life after three day and is now available in private devotions and weekly worship services for those who wish. Amen.

One aspect of the facts we face. One way of seeing things. Let us try another.

In the beginning was the Word and the Word was with God and the Word was God. He was with God in the beginning. Through him all things came into being, not one thing came into being except through him. John 1: 1-3 NRSV

In the beginning was Jesus! The Word, the Son! The pre-existent Christ! Who was with God and was God. Both at the same time. Jesus was with God, i.e. other than, not the same as, to be distinguished from, God. And yet he was God. Christianity has preserved the distinction ever since.

The pre-existent Christ is the one who created all things! Jesus was there all along. Before Abraham was Jesus says "I AM."

"John is it possible that *John's* community, isolated from earlier Christian communities, has taken a more mystical bent? Has perhaps read back into the tradition notions that reflect their uniquely inspired devotion to Jesus rather than the evangelical and ethically teachings of the synoptic gospels? Is it possible John's gospel is a neo-Gnostic interpretation of the Christian event?"

It's not just *John*. The other worldly mystical aspects of Christianity have been part of the mix since the beginning.

"He is the image of the invisible God, the firstborn of all creation; for in him all things in heaven and on earth were created, things visible and invisible, whether thrones, or dominions or rulers or powers - all things have been created through him and for him. He himself is before all things, and in him all things hold together." Colossians 1: 15-17 NRSV.

Colossians (above) and *Ephesians* and certain passages from Paul's more authenticated letters reflect a broad acceptance for the notion of the re-existent Christ. And of course the creeds as well.

"It's Mary again. I have a problem with "through him and for him.""

Yes?

"Doesn't Word or Logos in Greek mean Holy Wisdom and isn't Wisdom feminine? Sophia? And if that's true hasn't the feminine aspect of the Divine been neutered by patriarchal Christianity?"

Lord?

Yes John?

The Sophia group?

Briefly.

As a member
of a Sophia group
led by two Presbyterian
scholars, Reverend
Susan Cody
and Reverend
Hal Tassiq, I found comfort
and guidance
for several
years placing
my life in the
hands of
Sophia-Wisdom from whom all things were created.

During the two hour bimonthly classes we started by studying scripture, especially

Proverbs, Genesis 1 and *John 1* where as you stated there are feminine references to the Creator as the divine wind, Word, and Wisdom (Greek, Sophia).

Next we celebrated Sophia-Wisdom in art, skits, and periods of quiet meditation.

Sophia added a gentleness to my image of God that was missing in the judging Jesus worshipped by many believers. Sophia, though feisty at times (especially in *Proverbs*) reminded me of Jesus's nonviolent teaching on turning the other cheek and loving your enemies, which stood in stark contrast to the prevailing patriarchal Jewish and Greco-Roman culture in which Jesus lived.

"Are you still in the group?"

No. We parted on good terms. Their main interest was in the feminine aspect, Sophia; apart from, and even at times in opposition to, the authentically masculine aspect of Christ. I found myself restricted in my enthusiasm for the Christ that *John* and *Colossians* celebrated. Jesus, however his nature presents itself to us, is still the focus of the believing community.

***

"I find Christ in the elderly I work with. They are in a special place of knowledge."

Sheela Roberts

Jesus Again

Our baroque deity revived in modern dress
we reassess thy fading face;
icon of a bygone buried dust-dim dank and dark.

Dante nor Donne now etches icon on familiar field.
Shifting scene updated:
Jesus among the Gnostics, running with the rebels
plotting overthrow of Rome,
one more wonder worker dazzling the crowd.
Social worker rebel-prophet
all vie with the Risen One.
High Christology of John
sanctified by creed and council modified;
though Mark and others testified He had indeed
been seen among them after death.

Who knows at this late date what to believe?
Who cares?
Life oozes on precariously while Jesus fronts an ever-
changing scene
Apart like Mona Lisa's mien.

Kaleidoscopic context cloys; inkblot icon dim.
Seek Him!

Lines cross uncertain center to
divergent points of view arrayed around the rim.
Crucified again!
Praise Him!

***

"The overarching purpose of Trinitarian theology, and indeed of all theology...is the praise of God.. The language of praise is the primary language of Christian faith."

LaCugna

***

Father Fran Dorf's Sermon after the hymn exalting the greatness of our Savior God.

"Then doth my soul sing my savior God to thee… How great thou art."

Father Dorf, my beloved spiritual director for many years, said we were to pass on God's glory to our children and friends, just as the glory had passed from Jesus to his followers, then to Paul and on down to our own time. Like a family heirloom, say an expensive pearl, God's glory was passed from generation to generation. What struck me was that it was not a creed, a belief, not even the Sermon teachings, but the glory of God that was to be passed on.

Do our friends and family see in us the glory of God? Or only a set of beliefs and good deeds without the glory of God? What an inheritance we have to give our children, our grandchildren our friends and neighbors. What a treasure has been entrusted to us to savor and pass on to the whole wide world.

***

He was in the world and the world came into being through him; yet the world did not know him… *John 1:10 NRSV*

And today? The world still does not know him? With all the publicity about Jesus from thousands of Christian denominations, biblical scholars, even the media how can one say the world did not know him? Where is this Jesus that the world does not know? Still working as a gardener? Still on the street looking for a place to stay?

***

And the Word became flesh and lived among us, and we have seen his glory...full of grace and truth." *John 1: 14* NRSV

The coming into history of the pre-existent Christ puts us one step closer to the decisive event on which the pre-existent Christ and the other stables of Christian belief rest. One reads the gospel of John historically forward from the birth of Jesus (the Incarnation) through the early years and three years of public ministry to the culminating crucifixion and resurrection from the dead. As the Nicene Creed used at all Sunday masses puts it "He was born of the Virgin Mary and became man. For our sake He was crucified under Pontius Pilate. He suffered, died, and was buried. On the third day He rose again in fulfillment of scripture. Etc. Amen."

"So?"

So that's the official version. Which I believe.

"You said something about reading John's life of Jesus forward from the birth of Jesus to his death and resurrection. And then?"

Then we read *John* or any gospel, or any other New Testament work, backward from the Resurrection.

Without the Resurrection the other staples of Christian belief: the Incarnation, Holy Spirit, Trinity, coming kingdom of God etc. are open to serious question.

"For those who care."

As you say for those who care.

John?

Yes Lord?

Go ahead.

Let's start again and put the creedal beliefs in their proper place in the theological narrative. If one reads *John* from chapter one we're back at the beginning of creation with the pre-existent

Christ who after thirteen billion years steps into history as a burping, mewling infant. The one who was the Word, who was with God, who was God, steps into history as a human baby and grows into manhood. He works banging nails into wood in his father's woodworking shop, goes into hiding for a few years and then emerges as another Jewish itinerant preacher-prophet preaching about God's coming kingdom to bring relief from Roman oppression. In many ways his is a rather ordinary life. He makes friends with those who agree with his ideas and enemies of those who don't. Like other messianic preachers and miracle workers Jesus calls a few men (and women supporters) together to share his ideas on God's impending kingdom for which the Jews had been waiting for centuries. Like most of us his ideas aren't accepted. His friends turn away, but like other brave men he sticks by his beliefs and suffers for it. Finally...

"Can you move things along? Get to the point?"

That is the point. That's why the gospel is a *theological narrative*. A sacred story; a myth that according to Tolkein and C .S.Lewis happens to be true. Like other charismatic rabbis Jesus's message is suppressed by the authorities. Like many before him he suffers and dies on one of the many crosses spread across the small Roman province of Israel. One among many Jewish martyrs of his time Jesus's life and teachings would surely have been lost among the footnotes of history except for one singular event.

And then the event occurs on which all the rest depends. Jesus after being taken from the cross and put in a cave or some other burial place for several days, walks out of the cave and talks to one of his followers, a woman from Magdalene in a garden. The woman thinks he is a workman, a gardener in old clothes, and is amazed to see her old friend and teacher. Several others walking on the road talk with a stranger about the death of the latest messianic rabbi. Only after several hours of conversation do they recognize that the man they are talking with is the same man who had been sagging on a cross three days before.

Think of it! Your mother dies. You're there as she lies in bed and the breathing gets shorter and shorter and then stops. Her body comes to a rigid stillness and you say a prayer. Perhaps you are weeping. The following day you go to the funeral home and see her stretched out with a nice smile on her face. AND ONE DAY LATER SHE WALKS INTO YOUR HOUSE AND SITS DOWN TO EAT PIZZA!

That's it. That's what we believe. If we don't believe that the rest doesn't matter. Most of what Jesus said can be found in other places. The miracles are not unusual in the religious records. The quality of his life: forgiving enemies, caring for the poor, preaching on the need for repentance and turning to God, are all found here and there in other lives. But nobody walked through the door three days after being dead and began to eat pizza! Nobody.

***

"You said we read *John* forward starting from the pre-existent Christ, through the incarnation and..."

Ending with the crucifixion and the Resurrection? Yes. The historical perspective leads from the beginning, with the creation, through to the coming of the Messiah; his life, death and Resurrection. But the early followers' experience as Christians (and later the composition of the gospels) began with the Resurrection which led to a reconsideration of the birth of Jesus. Even to his role in initiating the creation thirteen billion years earlier. Unless the Resurrection is true it doesn't make sense to speak of Jesus being the pre-existent Christ.

Christian theology from beginning to end depends on that one event. I'm not saying many people aren't drawn to lead better lives by their association with Jesus as a prophet, role model for social change, or a symbolic figure for inner transformation.

"Mary here. But if the pre-existent Christ depends on the Resurrection of Jesus would it be fair to say that all things come from the Resurrection? Which would mean that an event well into human history is the initiating agent for the creation. Which doesn't make sense."

No it doesn't. The Resurrection is critical to illuminate the supernatural side of Jesus's person and mission but once Christ's nature has been revealed the believer need not dwell on only one aspect of his existence, but may allow the glory of God to unfold from one end of creation's history to the other. Once the gardener is unmasked we're invited to celebrate the presence of Jesus in all stages, and in all aspects, of the creation. Once I accept the Resurrection I can celebrate Christ-Jesus's role from beginning to end. From *Genesis* to *Revelations*.

"A compelling myth John but is it true? First Jesus got the dates wrong. The kingdom he promised "in this very generation" hasn't come yet. And second after two thousand years' things have gotten much worse. The planet is overcrowded with millions more refugees and other poor than ever before. Wars are no longer fought with swords but with drones, bombs, and the threat of weapons of mass destruction. Even your beloved Christians have pretty much given up on God's having a positive impact on history."

You forget Jesus was human. God-like ethically and spiritually, Jesus was limited by the knowledge available in his first century Hebrew Greco-Roman culture. He could be wrong about dates and times.

But you're right. There isn't much talk as there was in the Hebrew text of God raising up and casting down one nation one empire, after another. Today it's all peace of mind in a world at war and waiting for the end times when only true believers will be left to love their neighbors…

"And their enemies? Except of course there won't be any enemies because they'll all be in hell?"

Sin and the Saving Jesus

Jesus was, after all, the Savior; the one who forgives sins, who came to lift the burdens of the poor, to set the captives free, but what's the point of a Savior if everyone and everything basically stays the same? To believe in sin's defeat but expect the world to stay the same is a denial of Christ's ability to overcome sin, in whatever form it appears. If we argue for the power of grace to transform individuals why wouldn't we expect our sovereign God to use grace to transform the world around us? How can we assume that the tremendous inner changes God effects, are ineffective in confronting the evils around us? That God is God only of the inner devotional life but not of our engagement with the evils around us: social injustice, racism, and war.

"But didn't you say accepting the Resurrection of Jesus takes precedent over using Jesus as a role model for social change?"

For Christians yes. Even for the first Christians the teachings of Christ weren't enough. When Jesus was arrested all his followers fled, except for a few women and one male disciple who stood by him. The others had seen the miracles he performed. They'd spent three years listening to and trying to live out his teachings. The Sermon on the Mount was already etched in their minds so they should have known how to love their enemies, return good for evil; how to be peacemakers, the salt of the earth. They should have known how to face persecution when people reviled them and uttered all manner of evil against them on account of their association with Jesus. But the Sermon wasn't enough. They deserted Jesus.

Then three days after the crucifixion Mary Magdalene and a few other women, after fleeing from the empty tomb met Jesus who told them to tell the others that he was alive. The word spread. The Word spread! "He's alive! My God Jesus is alive! We're sorry. 0 Lord forgive us. You told us you'd be back but we didn't believe you. 0 Lord, we'll do anything for you. Please, give us a second chance. "And Jesus who asked others to forgive seventy times seven forgave the disciples. Took them back into his love.

"Except for Judas."

Except for Judas. A month or so later after Jesus had left them the disciples and Mary were given the gift they'd been missing; his own spirit, Paul's "Spirit of Jesus". And the Holy Spirit, empowered them to do what they had not been able to do, so that Jesus acting through his disciples carried and still carries out his own teachings. "Not I but Christ who lives in me," as Paul puts it.

As time passed all the scraps of Jesus' life were gathered together, treasured, and utilized in a life-style that distinguished them from the contentious world around them. For almost three hundred years until the coronation of Emperor Constantine in 325 C.E. to be a Christian was to follow the Sermon on the Mount.

Luke in the book of *Acts* calls the mix of faith and works the Way. Christians did not regard the teachings of Jesus as an unattainable political ideal, restricted to a domestic setting, as many Protestants do today; or as applicable to a select group of "religious" (priests, monks, and nuns) as many Catholics and Orthodox do, but they followed the Way of Jesus. They wouldn't serve in the army, or as jailers or judges sentencing criminals to torture and death. For almost three centuries Christians were sporadically hounded and beaten and fed to the lions because they stood out from the rest. They blessed rather than cursed their enemies, returned good for evil and would not take their beliefs underground during persecution like the Gnostics. But perhaps most importantly they wouldn't acknowledge the emperor as Lord, serve in his army, or in his courts[1]. Well past the reassessment of the imminent return of Jesus, late in the first century they continued to be part of God's kingdom. First fruits of the coming universal springtime.

***

Today there are two paths to salvation that rise above the controversial underbrush of New Testament scholarship. The first is the path of faith in the Resurrection of Jesus favored by most Conservatives, Evangelicals, and Fundamentalists. On the second path liberal, socially active Catholics, Quakers, and progressive main line Christians are motivated by the teachings of Christ especially the Sermon on the Mount. All Christians of course say they honor both faith and works but the emphasis is often on one path or the other.

While Jesus loves, comforts and guides both liberal and conservative Christians what if there were a fuller flowering of the glory of God in Christianity today? What if, as in the first three hundred years after Christ, Christians saw only one path? What if belief in the Resurrection empowered one to live out the teachings of Jesus, forgoing the ingrained strategies of avoidance

---

[1] A small number of Christians did however serve in the army. The extent to which Christians adhered faithfully to the Sermon is still being debated among Catholics, Protestants, Orthodox and the peace churches: Quakers, Mennonites, and Church of the Brethren.

and denial in order to learn the ways of peace, reconciliation, and service to the poor?

What if those who struggle to follow the teachings of Jesus in dealing with poverty, drugs, and the issues of war and peace were to turn - perhaps tired and worn from their efforts that seem so futile at times - to the one who first voiced those teachings in Galilee? Were to say, "Speak to me Jesus. Teach me who you are Jesus. I've admired your life, but I need more. I've tried to follow your teaching, to be your servant. Now I want to be your friend.

Another voice interrupts John's left leaning lecture. "What about the Crusades; the Inquisition. This rackles my cackles. Many Protestant ministers preach living the word."

Rackles my cackles?

"Rattles my cage. I just made it up."

Condense John.

We talk at cross purposes for several hours on Christian peacemaking. I'm surprised she's not more informed on the rationale and history of Christian pacifism while she challenges my bias against liberal Protestantism. I'm not uncertain about what I believe but I am worried I may have presented the case for Christian peacemaking too strongly. Am I driving away a good friend and sincere Christian who need to engage the gospel in her own way? Have I left little room for gospel as seed to grow at its own pace in each believer? Or am I simply afraid of being rejected for taking an unpopular stand on a vital issue?

***

Grandchildren Theology

The nativity scene was arranged on the big round table, just as it had been for ten years. Wise men on the right, shepherds and animals on the left, angels on the manger roof and the holy family just below welcoming the adoring visitors. But when I turned back from greeting Steve and Doreen little John had leveled the whole thing! The figures lay scattered on the round table, the manger had been dismantled, and straw was strewn everywhere.

Setting the scene up again I found myself putting the Christ child in among the other figures in a big circle where angels, wise men, animals and the holy family were all mixed together in no special order. I smiled, pleased that though my world just had been leveled, still, and Jesus had a part in the new circle which took its place.

Then John returned and began to move the figures again. This time he kept them standing, but when he'd finished playing the figures were left in what seemed to me, a quite random way. Just one big crowd with figures facing every which way. The Christ child was almost lost in among the taller figures, separated from Mary and Joseph who were off on the edge of the crowd with some sheep facing in opposite directions.

Next Christmas, just as I'd gotten used to the theological implications of the previous arrangements, John's younger sister Emily brought her own insights to the scene. This time the figures were carefully placed facing each other in pairs. Joseph was talking with the black king, Mary with one of the shepherds, and a large cow was bending over, in friendly conversation, with the infant Jesus.

Now, when I find myself stuck in one devotional pattern I'm reminded of John and Emily, and I begin to feel uneasy, wondering in what new form Jesus will present himself to me.

****

The Bread. I follow the bread of life like crumbs through the dark forest. .

The Wine. The cup of forgiveness. The blood of Jesus which flows in our veins making us one body. The body of Christ.

***

Holy Saturday. Walking among a hundred or so sisters at the large Jesuit center at Wernersville I stop one in the hall, looking for blankets from my liaison person. "I'm looking for Sister McCoy. "I'm Sister McCoy."... The tall thin priest raises his right hand and blesses the people with the only two fingers left on his right hand...The old nun's wrinkled face at perfect peace after the foot - well hand - washing... This is my church, this is the people I am part of. I love being married to you Lord with the wedding cross I wear. I love being a Roman Catholic. Why did you have to suffer so much Lord? ...

To draw attention to my suffering at being separated from the Father.

Suffering is not a ritual atonement to a fearful God of justice; but a wrenching separation between Father and Son. Between us and our loving God. It also uncovers the tension between power and love revealing that even without power God is love. That love is primary. That power, even to create, sustain and judge the entire universe, is secondary. God gives up the Son; allows the evil one to take the Son's life. Let's the evil one triumph over God. But even in defeat, even in suffering, God loves us through the Son who died in despair still loving God and his brothers and sisters on earth. Even his enemies.

Three days later Jesus comes back to love his sisters and brothers – without going straight to heaven to be with his Father. Think of it, Jesus chose us over his Father in Heaven. The Resurrection isn't about Jesus going home to God; it's about Jesus coming back to be with us. Only suffering love survives the onslaught of evil.

"Nothing really new there John. Christians have believed in love over power since the beginning. That's why Jesus was crucified."

If it *were* new I wouldn't trust it. ****

Embracing the cross during Passion Week is a Catholic means of grace. We not only say we believe in the creed, but we tell Jesus through embracing the cross, through kissing the wood, "We are sorry, we have sinned, forgive us, Lord." Not magic, but a means of grace; a place to let our hearts talk to God.

***

Wendy's and Myrna's wedding. Recalling our daughter's wedding where I stood nervously facing the guests gathered under the huge spreading cottonwood tree, with the cross and the picture of two women dancing behind me the phrases come back..."... that my words not detract from the love that is already here• .. 'nobody's business but our own' but now we celebrate the gift of private love in a public way... the gift of love, expressed through our feelings, our will, our bodies - with their wonderful erotic urges - comes from God. God makes lovers. God puts people together... Why love comes to any two people is a mystery. We can only celebrate its presence... glad Myrna and Wendy had the courage to accept this mysterious gift... Today they accept this gift in a special way. As Christians, as Catholic Christians, they ask Jesus, the Holy Spirit of Wisdom - Sophia - the Blessed Mary and all the angels and saints to bless and guide their lives together...

Especially they look to Jesus whose love was always greater than the love around him; whose circle of friends was always wider and more inclusive than the social borders of his time. This Jesus is still widening the circle. Still sending his love into the world in ways that have us stumbling to keep up... Lord Jesus bless Wendy and Myrna in their life together. Bless Father Richard Rohr and

Father Jack Robinson who at some risk lead our celebration. Bless all gay and lesbian couples that you've given the puzzling, challenging and wonderful gift of love... Let us also act with courage as Myrna and Wendy have, to not be ashamed or timid in our support of your gift of love. In the name of Jesus, our inner companion, our brother, our risen savior.

Amen."

***

Mass for three under the crypt at *S. Chiara* cathedral in Assisi. Room for just one beside two thin nuns on a twin prayer bench as the priest begins to read the gospel. In English! Tourists pile around us, hitting my feet as I withdraw to your presence... "I-give you the love that has no end."...

***

Just for Today (Tonight)

Lord I offer you my life just for today (just for tonight).
Bless me with your Holy Spirit just for today (just for tonight)
Bless me with thoughts of adoration for your sacred presence just for today (just for tonight).
Bless me with love for Betty and the people I meet in… just for today.
[Bless me with love for Betty and the people, figures and forces I meet in my dreams just for tonight].
Keep me Jesus in stillness and love just for today. (Tonight).

AFTERBIRTH

Stillborn, aborted, or born free of defects that would impede essential growth my words have been delivered. Having put the puppies up for adoption I can retire. And yet I wonder how they will fare in our uncertain world. Assuming they still live. Still whine and bark and yowl for their nocturnal home. Alone and parted from the rest, or were they taken in, two or three at a time, to bring solace to a shut-in nearing death, or to some squabbling couple struggling to channel colliding energies into routines of normal life. Perhaps "Love", or "God", or "Jesus" may yet act as such a gift to reunite the human family, center of the circle without end. Elusive Light Plato glimpsed illuminating seer and seen, observer and the world around us. Fulcrum on which the world wheels.

"And SELF? Would you care to weave that vicious cur into your happy tapestry of the playful canine family? Or why puppies might be an apt image for primal words?"

No. Analogies, like race horses must not carry too much weight.·

***

Some words: path, river, journey, life while not our final destination serve as stepping stones to elusive Truth. One must not as restless early medieval monks wandering from monastery to monastery be distracted from the heart's desire to settle for the fascinating endless search. Enjoying the interplay of what one takes to be aspects of the Truth one may miss one's last beginning; the word, no more than two or three, on which one's life depends.

***

If it's true human beings are finite beings predisposed to long for infinity primal words illuminate the elusive totality toward which we tend. Denise Levortov evokes the longing when she writes:

> *Something in us…*
> *hungers to offer up*
> *our specs of life's fragile tesserae*
> *toward the vast mosaic – temple, eidelon'*
> *to be ourselves embedded in its fabric,*
> *as if, once, it was from that that we were broken off*

***. .

* One star in *Baedeker's* travel guide indicates a site worthy of a visit.

** Two stars indicate a site of extraordinary interest.

Anywhere in creation is a one star site. Conversion, the Eucharist, a wedding or any worship service in a synagogue, church, temple, Quaker Meeting, or Pow-Wow, Da Vinci's *Virgin of the Rocks*, Cezanne's *Great Bathers* in Philadelphia, Beethoven's *Ninth* are all two star sites.

***

Mary Masseuse. "Hello? Can we leave off these culminating comments? For a few minutes there with Levertov's poem I had a nice sense of closure. I'd like to stay with that."

"John's what your closing word is?"

I love you guys. That's "the timely word" for me which *Proverbs* says "is like a golden apple on a plate of silver."

BIO

Facts that haven't been mentioned in previous bios include: I once shook hands with Dave Barry, as I write I'm torn between environmental commitments and the desire to cut down the leafy sycamore tree which is blocking my view of the Sandia mountains, I've been part of a Quaker Men's Group which has been meeting at least twice a month for almost forty years, Betty my wife at eighty eight is the same enchanting human being she was when we married sixty four years ago, I'm immensely proud of our five children and ten grandchildren, I miss friends who are no longer a phone call away, my favorite meal is lobster Newberg on toast with *Blue Nun* Riesling wine which I fantasize as a spiritual experience blending Catholic sensibilities and appreciation for an enhanced dining experience. You're right I may have mentioned Betty and the family before.

Primal Words: SELF, Love, God, and Jesus is John Corry's twenty ninth book. The reviews were mixed.

"I don't do interviews over the phone. No I haven't read the book"

French Deconstructionist Jacque Derrida.

"Needs work." Grouch Marx

"It is what it is." Yogi Berra

"Johnny's work has made its mark in contemporary literature. The great American mish mash." Mother

John Corry's intent throughout the twists and turns of the convoluted text is to evoke in the reader the ambiance of four primal words: SELF, Love, God, and Jesus. The first chapter Language in Labor sets the stage for four primal words which hopefully may inspire the reader to find their own primal words which lie half buried in the wealth of words that clutter up our busy lives.

Printed in the United States
By Bookmasters